Making *good* Career & *life* Decisions

You Have to Know **Who You Are** *to Get Where You're Going*

Making Good Career & Life Decisions
You Have to Know Who You Are to Get Where You're Going
Copyright © 1997 JIST Works, Inc.

This is a major revision based in part on work originally done by the staff of Northern Virginia Community College: Jacqueline Fribush Cooper, Steven Forrer, Jane Reimer Epperly, Jane Inge, and Joan Sibson Trabandt with contributions by J. Michael Farr, JIST Works, Inc.

Published by JIST Works, Inc.
720 N. Park Avenue
Indianapolis, IN 46202-3431
Phone: 317-264-3720 Fax: 317-264-3709 E-mail: JISTWorks@aol.com
World Wide Web Address: http://www.jist.com/jist

Interior Design by Kim Long

Printed in the United States of America

99 98 97 96   5 4 3 2 1

All rights reserved. No part of this book may be reproduced in any form or by any means, or stored in a database or retrieval system, without prior permission of the publisher except in case of brief quotations embodied in articles or reviews. Making copies of any part of this book for any purpose other than your own personal use is a violation of United States copyright laws.

We have been careful to provide accurate information throughout this book, but it is possible that errors and omissions have been introduced. Please consider this in making any career plans or other important decisions. Trust your own judgment above all else and in all things.

ISBN 1-56370-293-2

About This Book

This book is based on research done by staff of the Northern Virginia Community College. Their research asked the question: "What skills do adults need to get ahead in the workforce?" They found that certain skills DO tend to increase the earnings and long-term career success of those workers who have these skills.

The same staff then wrote several books that were designed to teach these skills to adults. This book and a similar one titled *Effective Strategies for Career Success* are revisions of those original works. While these revised books have been greatly modified and updated from the originals, they continue to teach essential skills needed for career survival and upward mobility.

Getting ahead in today's competitive workforce is no longer automatic. It takes more planning and effort than in the past. But it can be done. *Making Good Carrer & Life Decisions* and *Effective Strategies for Career Success* will give you important information that can give your career a long-term boost. We hope they help.

The editors and staff at JIST.

Part I Understanding Yourself

1. Who Are You — 3
- Knowing Yourself — 4
- Ingredients of Self-Awareness — 5
- Stereotypes — 5
- Self-Assessment Activities — 7
- Your Most Significant Experiences — 7
- Your Autobiography — 11
- Now What? — 12
- Checkpoint — 13

2. What Are Your Interests — 15
- Identifying Your Interests — 16
- Career Interest Inventory — 19
- Grouping Your Interests — 29
- Holland Cluster Chart — 31
- Getting More Information — 32
- Checkpoint — 33

3. What Are Your Skills? — 35
- Identifying Your Skills — 36
- Three Basic Types of Skills — 36
- Discovering Your Skills — 37
- Grouping Your Skills — 42
- Checkpoint — 47

4. What Are Your Values? — 49
- Identifying Your Values — 50
- Specific Values — 51
- Ranking Values — 52
- Can You Put a Price on Values? — 55
- Weighing Your Values — 56
- Checkpoint — 58

5. Defining Your Lifestyle — 59
- Identifying Your Present Lifestyle — 60
- Identifying Your Ideal Lifestyle — 61
- Checkpoint — 69

Part II Making Decisions

6. Decisions, Decisions — 73
- You Are a Decision Maker — 74
- Easy Decisions — 74
- What Is a Decision? — 75
- Levels of Decision Making — 76
- Areas of Importance — 76
- Identifying Levels — 79
- Where Are You? — 80
- Time Factors — 81
- Time Limitations — 81
- Your Goals — 82
- What Will It Cost You?
- What If You Had Made a Different Choice? — 83
- What Are the Odds? — 84
- How Much Risk Can You Accept? — 85
- You Can't Avoid Risk — 86
- Checkpoint — 88

7. Obstacles to Making Satisfying Decisions — 89
- Satisfaction Is Personal — 90
- Influences on Decisions — 90
- Determining and Defining Obstacles — 90
- Some Self-Defeating Statements — 91
- Internal and External Obstacles — 92
- Internal Obstacles — 92
- External Obstacles — 93
- Identify Your Obstacles — 94
- Take Charge of Your Life — 97
- Taking Control — 98
- Checkpoint — 99

8. Decision-Making Strategies — 101
- Living with Uncertainty — 102
- Decision-Making Myths — 102
- Avoiding the Usual Mistakes — 103
- Time Mistakes — 103
- Information Mistakes — 104
- Organization Mistakes — 105

Developing Confidence 106
Catch Yourself Doing Something Right 107
Praise Yourself 111
Get Help When You Need It 111
Where to Get Help 114
Checkpoint 116

9. The Step-by-Step Process — 117
Strategy and Tactics 118
The 7-Step Process 118
Example: Starting Your Day 119
Identify Your Situation—Then Change It 119
Three Kinds of Conflict 119
Conflicts of Interest 120
Expanding Your Options 121
Identifying Alternatives 122
Developing Alternatives 124
The Process in Action 126
Checkpoint 133

10. Using the Process — 135
Look at Your Past Decisions 136
Evaluation Charts 136
Make Your Decision 138
Summary Chart of Your Decision 150
For the Rest of Your Life 153
Checkpoint 154

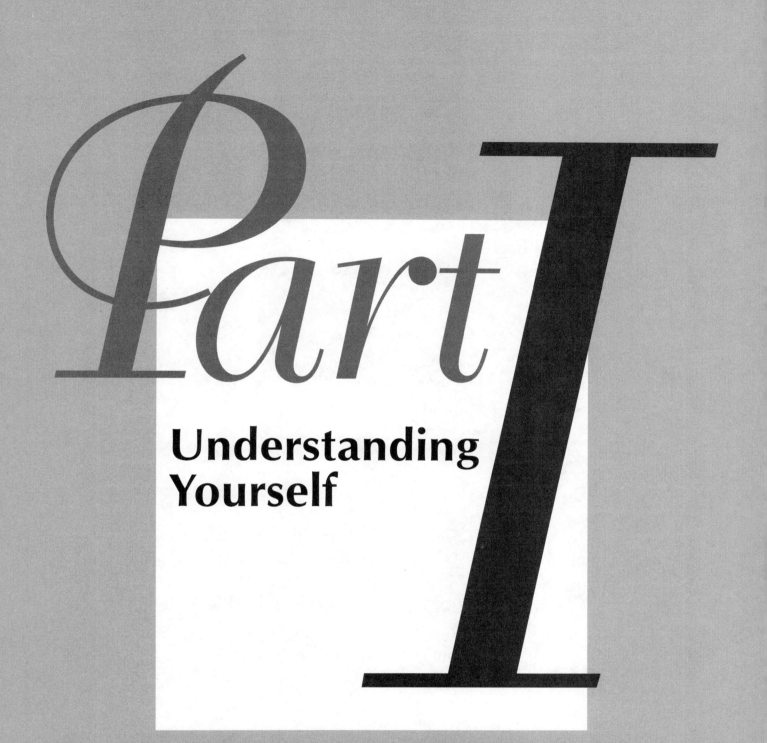

Part I

Understanding Yourself

Chapter 1

Who Are You?

➤ Key Point

Knowing who you are and what you need is vital when you are making major life or career decisions. This chapter presents several exercises that will help you identify your interests, skills, values, and lifestyle preferences.

As you complete the activities, be aware of stereotypes about what is appropriate behavior for someone based on age, gender, or race. Don't let these stereotypes limit your behavior or your goals.

Knowing Yourself

Try to answer the question, "Who are you?" Think of 10 different ways to answer. For example, you might say, "I am efficient," or "I am good with my hands," or "I am a musician." Your answers can include roles you play, beliefs you hold, responsibilities you have, groups to which you belonw, and interests you enjoy.

Who are you?

I am _____

I am _____

I am _____

I am _____

I am _____

I am _____

I am _____

I am _____

I am _____

I am _____

For most people, "Who are you?" is difficult question. Yet discovering who you are and what you want out of life is probably the most important step in the decision-making process. Unfortunately, many people skip this step when making major life decisions, maybe because self-assessment is often difficult and time-consuming. Knowing who you are and what you want out of life is the most valuable information you can have when making career choices.

Experts agree that work satisfaction depends on matching your personality with your work environment. As in all major life decisions, a thoughtful self-appraisal will help you make satisfying career decisions.

Working full-time means spending about 40 hours a week, 50 weeks a year, on the job—which adds up to 2,000 hours per year. How long will you be working? Ten years—20,000 hours? Fifteen years—30,000 hours? If you are 30 years old and plan to retire at age 60, your 30 years of work will equal 60,000 hours.

©1997 JIST Works, Inc., Indianapolis, Ind.

Considering the number of hours of your life at stake, the amount of time these exercises take to complete is negligible.

Think of something you dislike doing and picture it vividly. Then, imagine doing it for 8 hours a day, 5 days a week, 50 weeks a year. Do you get the picture?

Ingredients of Self-Awareness

What do you need to consider before making any life or career decision? It is most important for you to know your:

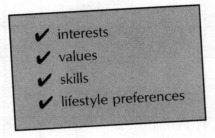

- ✔ interests
- ✔ values
- ✔ skills
- ✔ lifestyle preferences

These are the ingredients of self-awareness.

This book will give you the tools to assess eachy of these self-awareness factors so that you will be able to make more effective decisions about your career and your life.

Stereotypes

Before you begin your self-assessment, take a minute to think about assessing personal characteristics in general. Picture as clearly as possible a normal 65-year-old man, a normal 45-year-old woman, and a normal 25-year-old man.

Using your mental image of each of these people and the chart on the next page, describe the way you see each person. For instance, if you picture a normal 65-year-old man as someone who is rarely ambitious, you would place a check in the column opposite "Ambitious" and directly under "Less" in the 65-year-old man's column. Complete the form now.

How did you describe the 65-year-old man? The 45-year-old man? The 45-year-old woman? The 25-year-old man? Did you see them differently?

©1997 JIST Works, Inc., Indianapolis, Ind.

	65-Year-Old Man			45-Year-Old Woman			25-Year-Old Man		
	Less	Sometime	More	Less	Sometime	More	Less	Sometime	More
Ambitious									
Childlike									
Fond of Children									
Independent									
Strong Personality									
Absentminded									
Reliable									
A Good Decision Maker									
Inefficient									
Self-Sufficient									
Aggressive									
Competitive									

The generalizations you have about what is appropriate or typical behavior for men and women of various ages are called stereotypes. Everyone has stereotypes. To some extent, these generalizations are useful. They can help us make judgments about situations and people.

But no stereotype holds true for every member of a particular group—whether female or male, old or young, black or white, Christian or Jew, English or Polish. Stereotypes often result in inaccurate judgments about situations and people.

How do you see yourself? Do you see yourself as a stereotype of someone of your age, gender, race, and ethnic background? Do you censor things about yourself that don't fit this stereotype? Do you hold back from accepting some of your characteristics because "that's not the way you should be?"

This exercise has two purposes: first, to make you aware of the streotypes you hold; and, second, to encourage you to think about how stereotypes affect the ways you see (and possibly limit) yourself.

As you work through the exercises, be aware of stereotypes. Ask yourself this question: "Have I overlooked any of my interests, skills, or values because they don't fit with my own idea of what is correct behavior for me?"

Give yourself permission to accept parts of yourself that don't fit your stereotypes.

Self-Assessment Activities

The following exercises are designed to help you pinpoint who you are and what you need out of work and life. By reviewing your interests, skills, values, and lifestyle choices, you will be able to make better decisions.

You know yourself better than anyone else knows you, and learning what is important to you will lead to greater self-awareness.

You will be looking at the most significant moments from your life achievements and work experiences. From this exercise, you will produce the raw material needed to identify your interests, skills, values, and lifestyle preferences.

The remainder of this section assumes completion of this self-assessment. Many of the activities will use the information gathered from this first set of exercises. Be sure to complete it carefully before you move on.

Your Most Significant Experiences

DIRECTIONS: Complete these exercises one step at a time. Use extra sheets of paper as needed for this and other activities throughout this book.

In the blank spaces, list your achievements. Include anything you did well, felt proud of, and enjoyed doing—anything that was satisfying and meaningful to you. Be as specific as possible. For instance, instead of listing "gardening" as an achievement, say "planning, planting, and taking care of a vegetable garden last summer." Remember to limit your list so specific, time-limited achievements.

As you create your list, keep in mind that it doesn't matter what others think about these achievements or what rewards you received for them. For this exercise, only your opinions and feelings matter.

Try to make the list as long as possible. Focus on each 10-year period of your life, and try to list at least two achievements for each 10-year period.

©1997 JIST Works, Inc., Indianapolis, Ind.

Making Good Career & Life Decisions

Time Period	Personal Achievements

Select and list below the three most satisfying achievements of your life. Write the most satisfying achievement on the first line, the second most satisfying on the second line, and the third most satisfying on the third line.

Rank   Most Satisfying/Meaningful Achievements

1. _____

2. _____

3. _____

©1997 JIST Works, Inc., Indianapolis, Ind.

Using the chart that follows, list your top-ranked achievement in the left-hand column. In the right-hand column, break down the experience into the steps you used to achieve your goal.

List these steps as action statements. For instance:

Achievement	Step-by-Step Analysis
I jogged six days last week.	I decided I needed more exercise. I rearranged my schedule. I went to bed and woke up earlier each day. I forced myself to follow the plan no matter what happened . . .

Begin each statement with "I." Use action verbs (such as "rearranged") to describe what you did at each step. When writing your descriptions, be aware of the interests, skills, and values involved at the time.

Now, on your own paper, repeat the process for your own most satisfying achievements. Again, notice the interests, skills, and values involved.

Achievement	Step-by-Step Analysis

©1997 JIST Works, Inc., Indianapolis, Ind.

Briefly list all of your working experiences below. Be sure to include full-time, part-time, paid, and unpaid work. Don't forget work at home, community service, and volunteer work.

_____

_____

_____

_____

_____

Select the three major work experiences in your life. These must be the positions you most enjoyed that were of greatest importance to you. Remember to consider all of your work history when making your selections.

Rank   Most Satisfying/Meaningful Achievements

1. _____

2. _____

3. _____

STOP: It is important to complete this exercise before you go on with the rest of the book. Spending enough time now will enable you to discover your full range of interests, skills, and values. The insights gained and the upcoming exercises will help you to make more satisfying life and career decisions.

Take three pieces of paper. Write down a different major work experience at the top of each sheet. Thoroughly describe exactly what you did for that work experience. Remember, be as specific in your description as possible. Note the interests, skills, and values involved in each work experience.

©1997 JIST Works, Inc., Indianapolis, Ind.

Your Autobiography

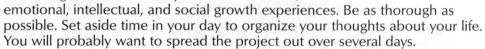

In this exercise you will make a chronological collection of your emotional, intellectual, and social growth experiences. Be as thorough as possible. Set aside time in your day to organize your thoughts about your life. You will probably want to spread the project out over several days.

Describe the kind of person you were and are today. What life events shaped you? Give some thought to what kind of person you want to become. Write in a free-flow style. Be sure to include your feelings along with the facts as you remember them.

If you have a very close friend or access to a tape recorder, talk about your life and its highlights before putting them on paper.

Start when you were very young. Try dividing your life into segments. These could be 5- or 10-year periods or even broader groupings, such as childhood, teenage years, young adult, family years, and adulthood. Do whatever seems easiest. You can start your autobiography by completing this sentence: "The thing I remember most in my preschool years is . . ."

This outline will be helpful as you write about your life segments:

I. Segments of life involved

A. People
1. Self
2. Family
3. Others

B. Experiences
1. Education
2. Occupation
3. Hobbies
4. Interests

C. Highlights
1. Accomplishments
2. Contributions
3. Important decisions
4. Failures

D. Feelings
1. Joys
2. Disappointments
3. Fears
4. Hopes

IMPORTANT: Before you start writing, read over the following Autobiography Checklist. Try to include each of these ideas in your writing. Check off areas on the list as you cover them.

Autobiography Checklist

- ❏ Your Feelings. How did you feel during each segment of your life? How did your feelings influence your work experiences and your relationships with others? Be sure to include your disappointments as well as your successes.
- ❏ Your Family Life. What family relationships did you have during this time period? How did they influence you?
- ❏ Other People in Your Life. What people were important to you at this time? What were their influences on your life? Whom did you most admire? Why?
- ❏ Your Life as a Student. How did you handle the course work? What subjects did you like? Which were your best? Which were your worst? Include activities outside the classroom as well.
- ❏ Your Jobs, Paid and Unpaid. Be very specific, and detail each duty performed on the job. How did you get along with coworkers? What were your feelings about your position?
- ❏ Your Hobbies and Interests. Were you involved in any organizations? What did you do in your spare time? What did you do for fun?
- ❏ Accomplishments. What made you feel proud? How did your accomplishments affect other areas of your life? How did they reflect on your relationships with others and your work experiences?
- ❏ Places You Have Lived and Visited. How have the places you have lived influenced your life and attitudes? What were your likes and dislikes about each? How do you feel about where you were and where you are now?
- ❏ Important Decisions. What were these decisions? What steps were involved in the decision-making process? Have you made any decisions you regret? Why?
- ❏ Ways You Have Matured. How are you different from other times in your life? When did your life's goals become focused? How have your life experiences influenced the goals you have made?

When you have finished reading this, set it aside for a day or two, and give the information time to "settle" in your mind before committing anything to paper. After you commit your life story to paper, you will be able to use the information throughout the rest of this book.

Now What?

Now that you have completed this chapter, you are ready to go on and identify your interests, skills, and values. These elements will have a direct bearing on any major life or career decisions you make.

Chapter 1 Who Are You?

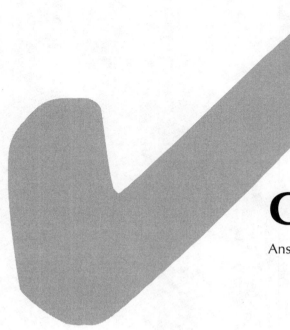

Checkpoint

Answer these questions:

1. Name the ingredients of self-awareness you should consider before making any major life or career decisions.
2. What are stereotypes?
3. How do stereotypes influence your perceptions of age, gender, and racial roles?
4. How do stereotypes affect the way you see your own behavior and life goals?

1. _____
   _____
2. _____
   _____
3. _____
   _____
4. _____
   _____

©1997 JIST Works, Inc., Indianapolis, Ind.

Chapter 2

What Are Your Interests?

➤ Key Point

The more your work and nonwork activities reflect your interests, the more likely you are to achieve work and life satisfaction.

The activities in this chapter will help you identify as many of your interests as possible, define your major interest patterns, rank these interests in terms of their importance to you, and determine ways you can pursue these interests.

Making Good Career & Life Decisions

Identifying Your Interests

Interests are usually easy to identify: They are the things you like. Some of these interests change over the years as you encounter new experiences. Others remain constant. Listing your interests can give you an eye-opening look at yourself and help you make major life or career decisions.

You might find it easy to name a few of your interests off the top of your head. But listing *all* of them will take some thought. One way to identify your interests is to use "Your Most Significant Experiences" activity from the previous chapter as a guide. Read Sandra Harris's story below as an example.

Describe Your Achievements

Sandra chose "making it on my own in Hollywood" as one of her most significant achievements. In describing that achievement, she said:

> "I decided school was not leading me anywhere. I enjoyed the newspaper work I was doing and considered looking for a job with a newspaper.
>
> "I had always been involved in school plays and was told I had talent. After I played the second lead in *Mame*, I realized I had to give acting a try.
>
> "I was intrigued by the people in acting and the self-discipline required to be a good actress.
>
> "I had no major responsibilities, so I decided to leave my friends and security for an unknown challenge.
>
> "I found that supporting myself was difficult. I had a string of jobs I didn't like: waiting tables, sales, and cashiering. Always being pleasant to so many people was hard. I was frustrated and motivated at the same time.
>
> "I learned photography from a friend and found watching my pictures develop very rewarding. I made some money taking wedding and baby pictures.
>
> "I met nice people who helped me out whenever I needed it.
>
> "I had three screen tests, but only one minor walk-on part.
>
> "I made it on my own supporting myself and pursuing what I wanted. I was very proud of myself."

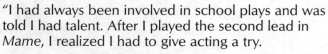
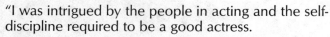

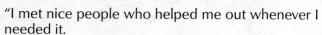
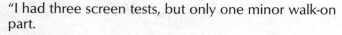
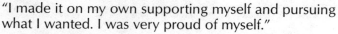

From her description, can you identify some of Sandra's interests? If she had written an autobiography, part of it might look like this:

> One of the most adventurous, carefree, and exciting times I ever had was when I left school at 20 to try to make it in the movies in Hollywood. Even though I was

©1997 JIST Works, Inc., Indianapolis, Ind.

enjoying my work on the college newspaper (for which I won a journalism award) and the acting I was doing, I didn't feel there was much direction in my other studies. I played the second lead in the school production of *Mame*, and I realized from that experience that I had to try professional acting. Everyone advised me against it, of course. But I was intrigued by actors and actresses. I decided to go anyway. I realized that I could always come back to my studies, but I might never again be as free of responsibility as I was then, at 20.

The two years in Los Angeles were the most exciting—and at the same time the most frustrating—period of my youth. The excitement came from the three screen tests I was given. There I was, in a motion picture studio, surrounded by camera operators and directors. Once I was even introduced to Katherine Hepburn. She really encouraged me to keep trying, even though it was hard at times to keep motivated. I supported myself with a string of jobs I didn't enjoy: waitress, salesclerk, and cashier. Being pleasant to so many people just wasn't for me.

Eventually, I started taking photography lessons from a friend who lived in my apartment building. He let me use his darkroom, and I loved spending hours alone, watching my photographs develop. When I was between jobs, I picked up money doing wedding and baby pictures. After two years and only one minor walk-on part, I realized I needed to make a decision about whether to stay or not . . .

In the spaces below, list as many of Sandra's interests as you can.

___	___	___	___
___	___	___	___
___	___	___	___

Does your list include these interests for Sandra?

- ✔ Adventure
- ✔ Journalism
- ✔ Acting
- ✔ Disciplined activities
- ✔ Photography
- ✔ Spending time alone

You can use your own experiences in the same way to uncover your interests. Reread your responses to "Your Most Significant Experiences" and "Your Autobiography." As you read, circle the phrases that indicate your interests. Then go back through the exercises and use the circled phrases to make a list of your interests. Keep in mind that your list will be much longer than Sandra's, which is based on only a small segment of her autobiography. Use the space on the next page to begin your list.

©1997 JIST Works, Inc., Indianapolis, Ind.

Complete List of Interests

_____

_____

_____

_____

Identify as many interests as possible. Remember, it's easy to overlook some of them. Get used to boasting about yourself. Be open to all the interests you find. Don't reject an interest just because it doesn't seem to fit with your idea of yourself.

Go back over "Your Most Significant Experiences" and "Your Autobiography" to look for interests. If you have skipped or rejected any, add them to your list now. While rereading, search for some of the following areas to find clues to your interests:

- ✔ Kinds of interpersonal relationships
- ✔ Religious activities
- ✔ Types of equipment
- ✔ Environments
- ✔ Education
- ✔ Hobbies
- ✔ Social activities
- ✔ Reading materials
- ✔ Repeated purchases
- ✔ Use of leisure time

To discover more of your interests, answer these questions:

- ✔ What do you read first in newspapers and magazines?
- ✔ What do you read for pleasure?
- ✔ What do you watch on TV?
- ✔ What kind of conversations do you most enjoy with your friends?
- ✔ What hobbies do you have?
- ✔ What events have excited you most in the last year?
- ✔ If you had the time, money, and energy to take any course you wanted, which course would you take?

©1997 JIST Works, Inc., Indianapolis, Ind.

Career Interest Inventory

This exercise will help you identify career areas and specific job titles that match your interests. If you already have a job objective, you can learn about related jobs you may have overlooked. What follows is a list of jobs organized into 19 clusters of related occupations. This list contains almost 200 of the most popular jobs in the United States. About two-thirds of all workers earn their living in these jobs.

> IMPORTANT: Mark each occupation with a check in one of the three columns. The three-letter code following each title will be explained later.

Consider each of the job titles in the list below. Decide the following for each occupation: Interested (I), Not Interested (NI), or Undecided (U). Check the column that indicates your choice.

Occupation	I	NI	U
Executive, Administrative, and Managerial Jobs			
Managers and Administrators			
Education Administrators (SER)			
Financial Managers (ESR)			
Health Services Managers (ESR)			
Hotel Managers and Assistants (ESR)			
Management Support Jobs			
Accountants and Auditors (RCS)			
Construction and Building Inspectors (CIE)			
Inspectors and Compliance Officers, Except Construction (RIE)			
Personnel, Training, and Labor Relations Specialists (EIS)			
Purchasers and Buyers (ESA)			
Underwriters (CSE)			
Engineers, Surveyors, and Architects			
Architects (IEA)			
Aerospace Engineers (IRS)			
Chemical Engineers (IRE)			
Civil Engineers (ISR)			
Electrical and Electronic Engineers (RIE)			
Industrial Engineers (EIR)			
Mechanical Engineers (RIS)			
Metallurgical, Ceramic, and Materials Engineers (IRS)			

©1997 JIST Works, Inc., Indianapolis, Ind.

Occupation	I	NI	U
Mining Engineers (REI)			
Nuclear Engineers (IRE)			
Petroleum Engineers (RIE)			
Surveyors (IER)			
Natural Scientists and Mathematicians			
Computer and Mathematical Jobs			
Actuaries (ISE)			
Computer Scientists and Systems Analysts (IER)			
Mathematicians (REI)			
Statisticians (IRE)			
Physical Scientists			
Chemists (IRE)			
Geologists and Geophysicists (IRE)			
Meteorologists (IRS)			
Physicists and Astronomers (ISE)			
Life Scientists			
Agricultural Scientists (IRS)			
Biological Scientists (IRE)			
Foresters and Conservation Scientists (RES)			
Social Scientists, Social Workers, Religious Workers, and Lawyers			
Lawyers (ESA)			
Social Scientists and Urban Planners			
Economists and Market Research Analysts (SCI)			
Psychologists (SIE)			
Urban and Regional Planners (ESR)			
Social and Recreation Workers			
Social Workers (SEA)			
Religious Workers			
Protestant Ministers (ASE)			
Rabbis (ASE)			
Roman Catholic Priests (ASE)			
Teachers, Counselors, Librarians, Archivists, and Curators			
Adult and Vocational Education Teachers (SER)			
Archivists and Curators (AES)			

Occupation	I	NI	U
College and University Faculty (SEI)			
Counselors (SER)			
Kindergarten and Elementary Teachers (SEC)			
Librarians (SEC)			
Secondary School Teachers (RCS)			
Health Diagnosing and Treating Practitioners			
Chiropractors (RES)			
Dentists (IRS)			
Optometrists (IRS)			
Physicians (ISR)			
Podiatrists (RSI)			
Veterinarians (IRS)			
Registered Nurses, Pharmacists, Dietitians, Therapists, and Physician Assistants			
Dietitians and Nutritionists (SIE)			
Occupational Therapists (SRE)			
Pharmacists (IER)			
Physician Assistants (IRS)			
Recreational Therapists (SEC)			
Registered Nurses (SIE)			
Respiratory Therapists (IRS)			
Speech-Language Pathologists and Audiologists (ISR)			
Health Technologists and Technicians			
Cardiovascular Technologists and Technicians (RCI)			
Clinical Laboratory Technologists and Technicians (EIS)			
Dental Hygienists (ERC)			
Dispensing Opticians (RCE)			
Electroneurodiagnostic Technologists (RCS)			
Emergency Medical Technicians (ESI)			
Licensed Practical Nurses (SEC)			
Medical Record Technicians (CSE)			
Radiologic Technologists (SRI)			
Surgical Technicians (ERS)			
Writers, Artists, and Entertainers			
Communications Jobs			

Occupation	I	NI	U
Public Relations Specialists (EAS)			
Radio and TV Announcers and Newscasters (ESR)			
Reporters and Correspondents (ESR)			
Writers and Editors (AES)			
Visual Arts Jobs			
Designers (AES)			
Photographers and Camera Operators (ESA)			
Visual Artists (AES)			
Performing Arts Jobs			
Actors, Directors, and Producers (AES)			
Dancers and Choreographers (AER)			
Musicians (AER)			
Technologists and Technicians, Except Health			
Engineering and Science Technicians			
Drafters (IRE)			
Engineering Technicians (IRE)			
Science Technicians (RIE)			
Other Technicians			
Air Traffic Controllers (SER)			
Broadcast Technicians (RSE)			
Computer Programmers (IRE)			
Library Technicians (ESI)			
Paralegals (SEC)			
Marketing and Sales Jobs			
Cashiers (CSE)			
Insurance Agents and Brokers (ESR)			
Manufacturers' and Wholesale Sales Workers (ESA)			
Real Estate Agents, Brokers, and Appraisers (ESA)			
Retail Sales Workers (ESA)			
Securities and Financial Services Sales Workers (ESI)			
Travel Agents (ECS)			
Administrative Support and Clerical Jobs			
Bank Tellers (CSE)			
Bookkeeping, Accounting, and Auditing Clerks (CRE)			

Occupation	I	NI	U
Computer and Peripheral Equipment Operators (CSR)			
Information Clerks (CSE)			
Mail Clerks and Messengers (SRC)			
Reservation and Transportation Ticket Agents and Travel Clerks (CES)			
Secretaries (CSE)			
Statistical Clerks (CRS)			
Stenographers, Court Reporters, and Medical Transcriptionists (CSE)			
Teacher Aides (SCE)			
Telephone Operators (CSE)			
Traffic, Shipping, and Receiving Clerks (CRS)			
Typists, Word Processors, and Data Entry Keyers (CSR)			
Service Jobs			
Protective Service Jobs			
Correctional Officers (SER)			
Firefighters (RES)			
Guards (SEC)			
Police, Detectives, and Special Agents (SER)			
Food and Beverage Preparation and Service Jobs			
Chefs, Cooks, and Other Kitchen Workers (RSE)			
Food and Beverage Service Workers (CES)			
Health Service Jobs			
Dental Assistants (ESC)			
Medical Assistants (SCR)			
Nursing Aides and Psychiatric Aides (SEC)			
Cleaning Service Jobs			
Janitors, Cleaners, and Cleaning Supervisors (REC)			
Personal Service Jobs			
Barbers (ESR)			
Cosmetologists (SEA)			
Flight Attendants (RIE)			
Preschool Teachers and Child-Care Workers (RES)			
Agricultural, Forestry, and Fishing Jobs			
Farm Operators and Managers (ESR)			
Mechanics and Repairers			

©1997 JIST Works, Inc., Indianapolis, Ind.

Occupation	I	NI	U
Vehicle and Mobile Equipment Mechanics and Repairers			
Aircraft Mechanics and Engine Specialists (REI)			
Automotive Body Repairers (RIE)			
Automotive Mechanics (RSE)			
Diesel Mechanics (REI)			
Farm Equipment Mechanics (RSC)			
Mobile Heavy Equipment Mechanics (RES)			
Electrical and Electronic Equipment Repairers			
Communications Equipment Repairers (RES)			
Computer and Office Machine Repairers (RES)			
Electrical Equipment Repairers (REI)			
Electronic Home Entertainment Equipment Repairers (RES)			
Line Installers and Splicers (ISE)			
Telephone Installers and Repairers (RCS)			
Other Mechanics and Repairers			
General Maintenance Mechanics (RIS)			
Heating, Air-Conditioning, and Refrigeration Technicians (REC)			
Industrial Machinery Repairers (RES)			
Millwrights (RES)			
Musical Instrument Repairers and Tuners (RCS)			
Vending Machine Servicers and Repairers (RCE)			
Construction and Extractive Jobs			
Bricklayers and Stonemasons (RSE)			
Carpenters (REI)			
Carpet Installers (REI)			
Concrete Masons and Terrazzo Workers (REI)			
Drywall Workers and Lathers (RIE)			
Electricians (RSE)			
Glaziers (RES)			
Insulation Workers (REC)			
Painters and Paperhangers (RSE)			
Plasterers (RES)			
Plumbers and Pipefitters (RCS)			
Roofers (REC)			

©1997 JIST Works, Inc., Indianapolis, Ind.

Occupation	I	NI	U
Sheetmetal Workers (REI)			
Structural and Reinforcing Ironworkers (REI)			
Tilesetters (RSE)			
Production Jobs			
Bindery Workers (RES)			
Blue-Collar Worker Supervisors (ESR)			
Boilermakers (RSE)			
Butchers and Meat, Poultry, and Fish Cutters (RES)			
Dental Laboratory Technicians (REI)			
Jewelers (REC)			
Machinists and Tool Programmers (RIE)			
Metalworking and Plastics-Working Machine Operators (RIS)			
Painting and Coating Machine Operators (RCE)			
Photographic Process Workers (RSE)			
Precision Assemblers (RES)			
Prepress Workers (RSE)			
Printing Press Operators (RSE)			
Shoe and Leather Workers and Repairers (RSE)			
Stationary Engineers (REI)			
Tool and Die Makers (RIE)			
Upholsterers (RCS)			
Water and Wastewater Treatment Plant Operators (RES)			
Welders, Cutters, and Welding Machine Operators (RES)			
Transportation and Material-Moving Jobs			
Aircraft Pilots (IRE)			
Bus Drivers (REI)			
Material-Moving Equipment Operators (REC)			
Truck Drivers (RSE)			
Handlers, Equipment Cleaners, Helpers, and Laborers (RES)			

©1997 JIST Works, Inc., Indianapolis, Ind.

Making Good Career & Life Decisions

In the space provided, divide your Not Interested occupations column into three individual subgroups. Create each subgroup according to your reasons for not choosing that particular occupation.

NOTE: A subgroup could be working with machines, selling products, being an assistant, or taking orders.

Subgroup I:

I would not choose the following occupations because:

_____
_____
_____
_____
_____

Subgroup II:

I would not choose the following occupations because:

_____
_____
_____
_____
_____

©1997 JIST Works, Inc., Indianapolis, Ind.

Subgroup III:

I would not choose the following occupations because:

For each of the three subgroups you just listed, turn your reasons for not choosing each into positive statements. For example, a subgroup of jobs that involves working with machines is sorted from the Not Interested group. A positive statement could be, "I am interested in working with people." List your positive statements here.

Subgroup I:

I am interested in:

Subgroup II:

I am interested in:

Subgroup III:

I am interested in:

_____
_____

Next, sort each of the occupations you selected as Interested into three "Might Choose" subgroups. Base these groups on your reasons you would consider each as an occupation you might choose.

Subgroup I:

I might choose the following occupations because I am interested in:

_____
_____
_____
_____
_____

Subgroup II:

I might choose the following occupations because I am interested in:

_____
_____
_____
_____
_____

Subgroups III:

I might choose the following occupations because I am interested in:

_____

_____

_____

_____

Now, turn back to your "Complete List of Interests" and add any other interests you discovered.

Grouping Your Interests

Look at your growing lists of interesting careers and related interests and identify the patterns within these lists. What major types of interests do they reflect?

Write your five major types of interests here. (Examples: athletics, helping people, scientific, artistic activities, working with ideas or numbers, working with machinery, etc.)

Rank	5 Major Types of Interests
1)	
2)	
3)	
4)	
5)	

A psychologist named John Holland noticed there was a relationship between what people were interested in and what kinds of job would suit them. From his research, he found that most interests could be grouped into one of six distinct categories. In each cluster, the interests that require certain skills and activities can be applied to many different occupations.

©1997 JIST Works, Inc., Indianapolis, Ind.

The Holland Chart summarizes the relationship between interests and jobs. Most people find that their own interests fit into one or more of these groups. As you look over the chart, think about which groups most accurately reflect your interests.

Carefully look at the Holland Cluster chart. Which three of Holland's six groups best describe your interest patterns? Rank these three groups by completing the chart below. Write the group that is closest to your interest pattern on the first line, and so on, until all three groups have been ranked.

Rank	Interest Patterns/Cluster Groups
1)	
2)	
3)	

Do the typical interests of the three chosen cluster groups describe your interests? No one group will encompass all interests or traits, but there is something of each group in all of us. Determining which of the Holland clusters you resemble most is a useful method of self-assessment, because this grouping process can simplify and order your list of interests.

Holland's research suggests that people are attracted to occupations that fit their interests, skills, and personalities. The better the fit, the greater your work and life satisfaction.

Enterprising (Code "E")
- **Personality Traits:** People who enjoy working with others—influencing, leading, managing for economic gain or to meet organizational goals.
- **Typical Interests:** Influencing others, selling, operating an independent business, giving talks, serving as officer of a group, supervising or managing others, meeting important people, leading others in accomplishing some goal.
- **Related Occupations:** Managerial & sales jobs, market analyst, banker, florist, TV announcer, personnel recruiter, contractor, lawyer, insurance underwriter.

Investigative (Code "I")
- **Personality Traits:** People who enjoy solving problems using mathematical and observation skills, and investigating, evaluating, and organizing information.
- **Typical Interests:** Working on scientific projects, taking courses in science, solving puzzles, using tools such as computers and microscopes, reading scientific books.
- **Related Occupations:** Doctor, astronomer, lab assistant, veterinarian, geographer, x-ray technician, electrical engineer, psychiatrist, medical technologist, computer operator.

Conventional (Code "C")
- **Personality Traits:** People who enjoy working with facts and numbers, following instructions, performing clerical, numerical, or other detailed tasks.
- **Typical Interests:** Keeping records, operating business machines, bookkeeping, being treasurer or secretary of organizations, timing auto races, using shorthand, working quickly.
- **Related Occupations:** Credit manager, office worker, medical secretary, payroll clerk, certified public accountant, ticket agent, typing teacher, proofreader, cashier, finance expert.

Artistic (Code "A")
- **Personality Traits:** People who enjoy using creativity, working with little supervision, using intuitive skills, solving problems imaginatively.
- **Typical Interests:** Writing, designing stage sets, playing in a band or orchestra, going to art galleries and plays, taking literature courses, singing with a group, dancing, choreographing, directing plays.
- **Related Occupations:** English teacher, script writer, craftsperson, illustrator, composer, graphic artist, dance instructor, public relations specialist, editor, fashion model, TV director.

Realistic (Code "R")

✔ **Personality Traits:** People who enjoy outside work, using tools and machines, using athletic or mechanical ability, working with plants and animals.
✔ **Typical Interests:** Woodworking, repairing appliances, building, gardening, reading blueprints, repairing cars, using mathematical skills.
✔ **Related Occupations:** Mechanical engineer, typesetter, fish and game warden, vocational arts teacher, surveyor, dental technician, tool and die maker, piano tuner, aircraft mechanic, forester.

Social (Code "S")

✔ **Personality Traits:** People who enjoy working with people, helping, training, curing, guiding, teaching, inspiring.
✔ **Typical Interests:** Volunteering for charity events, working on church committees, caring for children, planning parties, helping friends solve personal problems, dancing, sports events.
✔ **Related Occupations:** Training director, insurance claims adjuster, therapist, nurse, rabbi, librarian, social worker, food service manager, funeral director, physical education teacher.

Holland Cluster Chart

How well are your interests tailored to the occupations you are most attracted to? For an estimation, look back at the "Career Interest Inventory."

Review the occupational titles you checked in the Interested column. From these, select your 10 most-preferred occupations and list them, along with their three-letter codes, in the spaces below.

Ten Most Preferred Occupations	Holland Code
1)	
2)	
3)	
4)	
5)	
6)	
7)	
8)	
9)	
10)	

Each letter in the three-letter code represents a Holland Cluster. The first letter stands for the group that is most characteristic of the occupation. The second stands for the group that is second most characteristic of the occupation, and so on.

Some letters will occur more often. Do these letters match the Holland Clusters you selected as best describing your interest patterns? Remember, the greater the fit between interests and occupational choices, the greater your life and career satisfaction.

©1997 JIST Works, Inc., Indianapolis, Ind.

Getting More Information

The activities you have completed in this chapter should give you a good idea of the types of occupations that interest you. There are several ways to get more information on any of the jobs listed in this chapter, as well as on others not listed here. Here are some suggestions:

The *Occupational Outlook Handbook*: Most schools and libraries have a copy of the most recent edition of this important book. It is updated every two years by the U.S. Department of Labor and is a gold mine of information. All the jobs listed in the Career Interest Inventory on are described in the OOH. The descriptions include skills required, working conditions, future growth projections, training and advancement, average earnings, related occupations, and other details.

***The Complete Guide to Occupational Exploration*:** The CGOE is also available in most libraries. This book cross-references more than 20,000 job titles by skills required and in other useful ways. You can look up jobs that use skills and interests similar to ones you identified using the Career Interest Inventory. You will find there are many jobs that require a person with your skills and interests—not just a few!

***The Enhanced Guide to Occupational Exploration*:** The EGOE describes 2,800 jobs-that employ 95 percent of the workforce-and organizes them into 12 major interest areas with increasingly specific groupings of similar jobs. It is extremely useful for exploring career alternatives or for identifying job or educational options. General informaiton is provided for each grouping of jobs including the type of work; education, training, and skills needed; and other details.

The *Dictionary of Occupational Titles*: The DOT's 12,741 job descriptions are very specific and use precise language to describe specific tasks performed on the job. It's the kind of description that you might write if you actually observed the job being performed. This book, although large, is the best guide for specific job information, and virtually all career reference materials are cross-referenced to the DOT.

***The Career Exploration Inventory*:** This self-scored and self-interpreted assessment device requires the test taker to consider his or her activities in the past, present, and future by reflecting on 120 brief activity statements and indicate whether they like or would like to engage in that activity. The profile gives the test taker an immediate graphic picture of his or her interest level in 15 categories and related occupations.

The Library: Most libraries have all kinds of books and other information on the major career clusters. As you become more interested in types of jobs, the librarian can help you learn more about any particular job and ones related to it.

Other People: People who work in jobs that seem interesting to you are great sources of inside information. They can give you tips for getting started and help you decide if that type of job is what you really want.

NOTE: All of these career interest materials and many more are available at your local library, or can be ordered from the publisher, JIST Works, Inc., Indianapolis, Ind. Call our customer relations department at 1-800-648-5478 to place an order or request our current catalog.

©1997 JIST Works, Inc., Indianapolis, Ind.

Chapter 2   What Are Your Interests?

Checkpoint

Answer these questions:

1. Which Holland Clusters best describe your interests?
2. What are your major interest patterns? Which are your strongest interests?
3. How are you satisfying those interests?
4. What are other ways to pursue those interests?

1. _____

2. _____

3. _____

4. _____

©1997 JIST Works, Inc., Indianapolis, Ind.

Chapter 3

What Are Your Skills?

➤ Key Point

Evaluating your skills is the toughest part of self-assessment. Many people think they have few skills and overlook many of the skills they do have. The activities in this chapter will help you identify and group your skills.

Identifying Your Skills

A skill is an ability to do something. Examples of skills include such things as natural abilities—knacks for doing certain things—special talents, and acquired training or know how.

Everyone has hundreds of skills. But most people overlook many of them. This is especially true of skills that are second nature or skills learned early in life. The exercises in this chapter will help you uncover and recognize important skills you may have overlooked.

Three Basic Types of Skills

Work and Activity Skills

These skills are related to the things you have done in a particular work or activity (paid or nonpaid).

- ✔ Typing legal documents
- ✔ Bowling
- ✔ Gardening
- ✔ Preparing lesson plans
- ✔ Repairing cars
- ✔ Knowing the names of all the muscles in the human body
- ✔ Operating a cash register
- ✔ Decorating a house
- ✔ Tailoring suits
- ✔ Cutting or styling hair
- ✔ Directing traffic
- ✔ Pumping gas
- ✔ Taking blood pressure

General Skills

These are related to people, data, and things that can be used in many different situations.

Dealing with people:
- ✔ Communicating
- ✔ Negotiating
- ✔ Human relations
- ✔ Teaching
- ✔ Supervising
- ✔ Persuading
- ✔ Performing
- ✔ Leading

Dealing with data
- ✔ Developing and planning
- ✔ Organizing
- ✔ Analyzing
- ✔ Innovating
- ✔ Researching
- ✔ Computing
- ✔ Comparing
- ✔ Numerical and financial
- ✔ Managing

Dealing with things
- ✔ Precision working
- ✔ Operating
- ✔ Tending
- ✔ Machine and manual skills
- ✔ Handling
- ✔ Artistic

Personal Skills

These skills involve self-control when dealing with people and time.

- ✔ Punctual
- ✔ Dependable
- ✔ Conscientious
- ✔ Congenial
- ✔ Efficient
- ✔ Imaginative
- ✔ Industrious
- ✔ Leadership ability
- ✔ Loyal
- ✔ Open-minded
- ✔ Patient
- ✔ Persistent
- ✔ Sincere
- ✔ Sympathetic
- ✔ Tolerant
- ✔ Athletic

Discovering Your Skills

On the following page record as many skills as possible. Look for all three types of skills: Work and Activity Skills, General Skills, and Personal Skills. The objective of each activity is to add to your list of skills.

REMEMBER: *You have hundreds of skills. All you need to do is recognize them.*

Making Good Career & Life Decisions

Complete List of Skills

Work and Activity Skills

_____

_____

_____

_____

_____

General Skills

_____

_____

_____

_____

_____

Personal Skills

_____

_____

_____

_____

_____

©1997 JIST Works, Inc., Indianapolis, Ind.

List the answers to "Who Are You?" from the first chapter in the spaces provided. For each definition, list at least one needed skill. If one answer was "homemaker," you might list financial management as a skill. Add these skills to your "Complete List of Skills."

Who Are You?

I am	_____
Skill	_____
I am	_____
Skill	_____
I am	_____
Skill	_____
I am	_____
Skill	_____
I am	_____
Skill	_____
I am	_____
Skill	_____
I am	_____
Skill	_____

Interests often lead to developing skills. List the answers to "5 Major Types of Interests" in the spaces that follow. Then list at least three skills you use in pursuing each interest. Remember to include general and personal skills, as well as the specific work and activity skills. Add these skills to your "Complete List of Skills."

©1997 JIST Works, Inc., Indianapolis, Ind.

Five Major Interests

1. _____
   _____
   _____

2. _____
   _____
   _____

3. _____
   _____
   _____

4. _____
   _____
   _____

5. _____
   _____
   _____

Refer to "Your Most Significant Experiences" earlier. Analyze each achievement and work experience for work and activity, general, and personal skills. For example, consider the sample used for the following Achievement Analysis Chart.

The skills used include decision making, efficient use of time, self-control, perseverance, organization, and planning. As you analyze each of your achievements and work experiences, add any new skills to your "Complete List of Skills."

Review your autobiography for clues to work and activity, general, and personal skills. Again, add any additional skills to your "Complete List of Skills."

©1997 JIST Works, Inc., Indianapolis, Ind.

Sample Achievement Analysis Chart				
Achievement	**Step-by-Step Process**	**Work/Activity**	**General**	**Personal**
I jogged six days last week.	I decided I needed more exercise. I rearranged my schedule. I went to bed and woke up earlier each day. I forced myself to follow the plan no matter what happened . . .	Rearranged schedule Set alarm clock	Decision-making Organizing Analyzing Efficient use of time Planning	Self-control Efficient Industrious Persistent Perserverence

Sample Achievement Analysis Chart				
Achievement	**Step-by-Step Process**	**Work/Activity**	**General**	**Personal**

©1997 JIST Works, Inc., Indianapolis, Ind.

Grouping Your Skills

KEEP IN MIND: There are many ways and areas in which you can use these skills, including your job, leisure time, family life, as a consumer, or in the community. Look at all aspects.

After you have determined the long list of skills that shows your talents, go back and look over what you have discovered. Review your "Complete List of Skills," then answer the following questions in the spaces provided.

What skills did you already know about?

_____
_____
_____
_____
_____

What skills did you discover you had?

_____
_____
_____
_____
_____

What five skills do you enjoy using the least?

Five Skills I Least Enjoy

1. _____
2. _____
3. _____
4. _____
5. _____

What five skills do you enjoy using most?

Five Skills I Enjoy Most

1. _____
2. _____
3. _____
4. _____
5. _____

For the five skills you enjoy most, list ways you are using them.

Ways I Am Using Skills I Enjoy Most

1. _____
2. _____
3. _____
4. _____
5. _____

Brainstorm and list possible ways of using the five skills you most enjoy.

Possible Ways of Using These Skills in the Future

1. _____
2. _____
3. _____
4. _____
5. _____

Look again at your "Complete List of Skills." What skills are repeated again and again?

_____
_____
_____

To what extent do these skills relate to people, data, or things?

_____
_____
_____

Can you identify any other patterns in your skills lists?
(For example, organizing, interpersonal, or machine-related skills.)

_____
_____
_____

With the answers to the previous series of questions, organize your skills into five groups of common themes. For example, communication skills would include negotiating, teaching, persuading, and listening. Review the examples of general skills and the Holland Clusters. Use these as a guide for grouping your skills.

Skill Group One Theme: _____

Skills:
_____
_____
_____
_____
_____
_____
_____

Skill Group Two Theme: _____

Skills:
_____
_____
_____
_____
_____
_____
_____

Skill Group Three Theme: _____

Skills:
_____
_____
_____
_____
_____

Skill Group Four Theme: _____

Skills:
_____
_____
_____
_____
_____

Skill Group Five Theme: _____

Skills:
_____
_____
_____
_____
_____

Chapter 3 What Are Your Skills?

Checkpoint

Answer these questions:

1. What are skills?
2. What work and activity, general, and personal skills do you have?
3. Which Holland Clusters best describe your skills?
4. Which are your strongest skills?

1. _____

2. _____

3. _____

4. _____

©1997 JIST Works, Inc., Indianapolis, Ind.

Chapter 4

What Are Your Values?

➤ Key Point

One of the most important factors in making decisions is your value system. In this chapter you will explore, evaluate, and rank the things that are important to you.

Identifying Your Values

Values are the ideals you strive for in your day-to-day behavior: the things you believe in, spend time on, and would fight for.

Your values are the result of many influences learned through rules and examples. Probably the most important sources are your parents and family. Whenever you make a choice, you unconsciously rank your values. Making a choice strengthens the importance of that value to you and directs your behavior.

You may find it easy to identify your values. They represent the big occasions, important feelings, and significant relationships in your life. These values will probably influence your future actions.

Reread "Your Most Significant Experiences" and "Your Autobiography." Underline the phrases that represent your values. Use the space below to make a list of your values.

IMPORTANT: Check carefully for clues to your values, such as major accomplishments, significant feelings, and attitudes. Include all your values. Don't reject any.

Complete List of Values

_____

_____

_____

_____

_____

_____

_____

_____

_____

Specific Values

How do you identify specific values? Read the following statements and try to match each with a value listed in the box that follows. Write the appropriate letter in the spaces below.

1. _____ I remember the joy and pride at the family party when I was the first to graduate from business school.

2. _____ When my children brought me completed homework assignments, I always rewarded them with . . .

3. _____ I love the Mexican holiday traditions, foods, and folklore my grandmother taught me.

4. _____ One of the things I liked most about my twenties was the lack of ties and responsibilities. It gave me a feeling of . . .

5. _____ I enjoyed being part of the old neighborhood gang. On Saturday nights, we would . . .

6. _____ I've always tried to get as much done as possible because there are so many things I want to do, and yet . . .

7. _____ During the week, I spend a great deal of time—probably two or three hours a day—planning what to wear, preparing my clothes, and getting myself ready.

8. _____ I was angry and disappointed when Jamie used my idea to win a big project without giving me credit. So, in my dealings with my coworkers, I always try to be . . .

9. _____ I remember that year well because I got a raise and was able to buy a newer car.

10. _____ I was so excited about seeing her after all these years that I left the restaurant without paying the check. I didn't think about it until the end of the day. Then I went back and paid it.

11. _____ The first day of my promotion was glorious. I got a private office with my name on the door and a new title. I got a big kick out of telling people my job title.

12. _____ He had been the best friend I'd ever had. When I found out he'd been telling other people the things I'd told him in confidence, I just didn't want to see him anymore.

13. _____ The new minister immediately began setting up new programs for the teenagers and older members of the church. The whole congregation felt a sense of rebirth. I have never felt so close to the true meaning of life.

14. _____ Even though it was a good job, I just couldn't work any more for a company that had so little regard for preserving the environment.

15. _____ That year I got a two-week vacation. Our neighbors invited us to go with them to the beach, but we decided to visit my parents instead.

©1997 JIST Works, Inc., Indianapolis, Ind.

> **Values**
>
> A. Acceptance
> B. Loyalty
> C. Fairness
> D. Material possessions
> E. Independence
> F. Religious beliefs
> G. Creativity
> H. Personal appearance
> I. Time
> J. Social consciousness
> K. Education
> L. Heritage
> M. Family
> N. Honesty
> O. Status

Ranking Values

Use the following exercises to identify other values you hold. The values that take more thought to uncover may be the ones that give you new insight. After completing each exercise, add the new-found values to your "Complete List of Values."

Rank your choice for each of the following questions by placing a 1, 2, or 3 next to the statement. Identify the values implied by the choices you make, and write your answer in the spaces below.

1. If you inherited $15,000, how would you use it?

   ____ Start a business
   _____

   ____ Travel
   _____

   ____ Save it
   _____

2. If you caught your friend telling others a lie, what would you do?

   ____ Tell the truth
   _____

   ____ Keep silent
   _____

   ____ Question your friend later
   _____

©1997 JIST Works, Inc., Indianapolis, Ind.

3. How would you want most of your tax money spent?

____ Cancer research

_____

Country's defense

_____

____ Economic equality

_____

4. What do you most enjoy?

____ Being alone

_____

____ Being with one or two friends

_____

____ Being with many people

_____

5. If you were asked to volunteer for a committee office, which would you choose?

____ President

_____

____ Historian

_____

____ Treasurer

_____

6. What would you most like to change?

____ Your leisure time activities

_____

____ Your physical appearance

_____

____ Your personality

_____

©1997 JIST Works, Inc., Indianapolis, Ind.

7. If you had a week's vacation, how would you spend it?

____ Alone

____ With a friend

____ With your family

8. If you were married and were offered an unbeatable job in another town, what would you do?

____ Commute on weekends

____ Move your family to the new town

____ Turn down the offer

9. Which work would you like the best?

____ Work you really like with low pay and high status

____ Work that is dull with high pay and high status

____ Work you really like with high pay and low status

10. What would you do to be promoted?

____ Turn in a coworker's idea as your own

____ Wine and dine the boss

____ Lie about your qualifications

11. If you found your friend worked for a company involved in chemical warfare, which you violently oppose, how would you handle it?

____ Pay no attention

©1997 JIST Works, Inc., Indianapolis, Ind.

___ End the friendship

___ Try to talk your friend into leaving the company

12. Which would you rather give up?

___ The right to vote

___ The right to free speech

___ The right to religious choice

Answers for "Specific Values."	1. K	4. E	7. H	10. N	13. F
	2. G	5. A	8. C	11. O	14. J
	3. L	6. I	9. D	12. B	15. M

Can You Put a Price on Values?

Imagine you are attending an auction of lifetime values, and the auctioneer has listed a price for each value. (These prices are arbitrary and have nothing to do with your values.) You have $2,000 in cash in your pocket. These are once-in-a-lifetime purchases. What values would you buy with your $2,000? Write your choices in the space provided.

Value Price List

Acceptance	$200	Freedom	$200	Equality of the sexes	$300
Loyalty	100	Courage	200	Equality of races	300
Fairness	100	Success	300	Tolerance	200
Material possessions	300	Pride	200	Patriotism	300
Independence	200	Love	100	Justice	200
Religious beliefs	300	Sexual ability	300	Adventure	200
Creativity	300	Morality	200	Security	100
Beauty	300	Power	300	Self-discipline	200
Time	200	Serving others	200	Respect	300
Awareness of social issues	200	Truth	100	Dignity	200
Education	100	Friendship	100	Nature	300
Heritage	200	Politics	200	Productivity	200
Family	200	Work	200	Efficiency	100
Honesty	200	Leisure time	200	Competition	200
Status	200	Culture	200	Personal recognition	200
Health	300	Peace	100	Obedience	200
Life	300	Authority	100	Happiness	300
Cleanliness	200	Generosity	300	Responsibility	100

©1997 JIST Works, Inc., Indianapolis, Ind.

Value	Price
_____	_____
_____	_____
_____	_____
_____	_____
_____	_____
_____	_____
_____	_____
_____	_____

Moral Dilemma: A person across the room bids $1,999 for one of the values you want most. Will you give it up or spend your whole $2,000 for it?

Look over your responses in the last few pages and add to the "Complete List of Values" any values not already there.

Weighing Your Values

At this point, you have a good idea of the things that are important to you. However, you may not be able to tell which of these values has the most influence on your life. New issues are constantly affecting or changing our values. You should take stock of your values when you and they appear to be changing. You can use the following three methods to measure the strength of your values.

Choosing: Values result from making a choice between different attitudes or behaviors after thoughtful consideration of all alternatives. An attitude or behavior becomes a value only if you have freely chosen it. An example of this would be choosing to go to a family picnic rather than going fishing with friends.

Prizing: Values are cherished and important. You are proud of them and do not hesitate to state or defend them in public. For example, you defend your choice of a family picnic over fishing, despite kidding from your friends.

©1997 JIST Works, Inc., Indianapolis, Ind.

Acting: Values are usually visible in your daily life. You react to situations in ways that are compatible with your values. In this way, you form a consistent pattern. Again, you would prefer family activities on a day-to-day basis.

Go back over your "Complete List of Values" and choose the 10 values that are most important to you. Write them in the spaces below. Place the value with the most importance in space number 1. Write the next most important value in space number 2, and so on, until all 10 have been ranked.

As you do this, weigh the strength of each value by considering how much you would choose, prize, and act on it. Ask these questions:

Have you chosen it?

Are you proud enough of this value to defend it in public?

Do you act on it in some way every day?

Rank	Value
1	
2	
3	
4	
5	
6	
7	
8	
9	
10	

Checkpoint

Answer these questions:

1. What are my major values?
2. Which values are most important to me?
3. How am I expressing these values in my everyday life?
4. What other activities might I pursue to better express my most important values?

1. _____
   _____

2. _____
   _____

3. _____
   _____

4. _____
   _____

Chapter 5

Defining Your Lifestyle

► *Key Point*

Now that you have analyzed your interests, skills, and values, what can you do with the information?

With the activities in this chapter you will define your ideal lifestyle based on your unique combination of interests, skills, and values. Knowing what type of lifestyle best suits you will help you make better decisions in all areas of your life.

Identifying Your Present Lifestyle

Lifestyle is how you live your life. Your present lifestyle can be identified by the way you spend your time.

How much of your time is spent working, pursuing leisure activities, being with your family, participating in community activities, and handling routine matters? In the space below, describe what you do each hour of the day. Be specific in describing your daily activities.

If there are any interests, skills, or values you are not expressing that you would like to, it is important to investigate your present lifestyle. Your satisfaction with your life will be greatest when your lifestyle preferences are in keeping with your interests, skills, and values.

Your lifestyle preferences will always involve compromises. For example, you live in an apartment but, at the same time, want to have a vegetable garden. This conflict could be resolved by renting a garden plot somewhere else or growing indoor varieties of vegetables.

Time	Typical Weekday	Typical Weekend/Holiday
7:00 a.m.		
8:00		
9:00		
10:00		
11:00		
12:00		
1:00 p.m.		
2:00		
3:00		
4:00		
5:00		
6:00		
7:00		
8:00		
9:00		
10:00		
11:00		
12:00 a.m.		

©1997 JIST Works, Inc., Indianapolis, Ind.

Identifying Your Ideal Lifestyle

Your ideal lifestyle should be based on your unique combination of interests, skills, and values. No two people will have the same combination of factors, and no two lifestyles will be exactly the same. Knowing what type of lifestyle best satisfies your interests, skills, and values will help you make better life and career decisions.

What is your ideal lifestyle? The following exercise will help you decide. This inventory lists 21 elements of lifestyle. Each element describes the two extremes of a lifestyle preference. For instance, some people would rather live alone while others prefer to be part of a family or group of friends. Both extremes are equally acceptable. Remember, there are no right or wrong answers. For each element, check the box that best describes your preference.

For example, if you think it is very important for you to live alone, you would check the "Very Important" box next to the "Live Alone" category. If it does not matter to you whether you live in a rural area or an urban area, you would check the box under "Not Important" for that category.

Ideal Lifestyle Inventory						
	Very Important	Somewhat Important	Not Important	Somewhat Important	Very Important	
live alone						live with people
live in rural area						live in urban area
live in house						live in apartment
own living quarters						rent living quarters
have children						have no children
entertain at home						go out for entertainment
spend money						save money
frequent travel						little or no travel
have many possessions, luxuries						little need for possessions, luxuries
have large sums of money						little need for large sums of money
live close to recreational facilities						little need for recreational facilities

©1997 JIST Works, Inc., Indianapolis, Ind.

Ideal Lifestyle Inventory

	Very Important	Somewhat Important	Not Important	Somewhat Important	Very Important	
active religious life						little need for religious activities
live in cultural centers (e.g., theatre, ballet, concerts)						little need for cultural stimulation
political activity						little need for political activity
access to public entertainment (e.g., movies, restaurants)						little need for public entertainment
active member in community						little need for tight nit community
time alone						time surrounded by people
access to educational facilities (e.g., schools, libraries)						little need for educational facilities
live in constant climate						live in seasonal climate
live near place of work						live 1/2 hour or more from place of work
work only for wages						work is central focus of life

Rick Smith

As an example, look at what Rick Smith has identified as his five most important interests, skills, and values. He has also identified the activities he would most like to use to express those interests, skills, and values.

There are many different ways Rick could combine his interests, skills, and values. Because he likes mathematics, computers, and young people, he could be a computer science instructor at the local community college. He could be active in his community through statistical analysis consulting for his local political party or coaching the YMCA's swim team. His concern for health will probably keep him on a regular exercise program. He enjoys spending time with his family, and will probably keep his weekends free for family outings. He might also save some of his leisure time for buying, building, and repairing stereos.

	Interests	Activities
1	Athletics	Coach Swim Team
2	Social	Working with young people
3	Mathematics	Working with computers
4	Music	Building and repairing stereos
5	Enterprising	Statistical analysis consulting

	Interests	Activities
1	Supervising	Working with young people
2	Industrious	Working on stereos
3	Computing	Occupation
4	Knowledge of math	Computer work
5	Conscientious	In all areas

	Interests	Activities
1	Health	Physical exercise
2	Family	Weekend outings
3	Time	Use to do things I like
4	Responsibility	Economically self-sufficient
5	Education	Saving money for it

©1997 JIST Works, Inc., Indianapolis, Ind.

Using the information you gathered in earlier chapters, think about how you might incorporate your own major interests, skills, and values into your present lifestyle.

Write in the following spaces your five most important interests, skills, and values. In the blank to the right of each, write the activity you would most like to use to express that interest, skill, or value. For example, tennis is one of your five most important interests. You could express your interest by teaching tennis to children. So you would write "tennis" and "teaching children" in the appropriate boxes in the interests block.

	Interests	Activities
1		
2		
3		
4		
5		

	Interests	Activities
1		
2		
3		
4		
5		

	Interests	Activities
1		
2		
3		
4		
5		

Below, describe how you might change your present lifestyle to include the activities related to the major interests, skills, and values you listed.

With your five most important interests, skills, and values in mind, consider the following questions for additional insight into your lifestyle preferences, and write your answers in the space provided.

Can you think of any organizations that might pay you to do the things you have described?

_____
_____
_____
_____
_____
_____
_____

Did you learn anything new about your ideal lifestyle?

_____
_____
_____
_____
_____
_____
_____

Chapter 5 Defining Your Lifestyle

What three things are essential for your ideal lifestyle?

1. _____
2. _____
3. _____

Now list those things you would most like to change about your present lifestyle.

Making Good Career & Life Decisions

What will you have to do to bring about these changes?

IT'S UP TO YOU: With the information you've gathered so far, you will be able to take fuller advantage of any major life or career decisions that come along, because you know who you are and what you want out of life. In the next section you will learn a process to help you make better lifelong decisions.

Chapter 5 Defining Your Lifestyle

Checkpoint

Answer these questions:

1. What is your present lifestyle?
2. How would your ideal lifestyle differ?

1. _____
   _____
   _____
   _____

2. _____
   _____
   _____
   _____

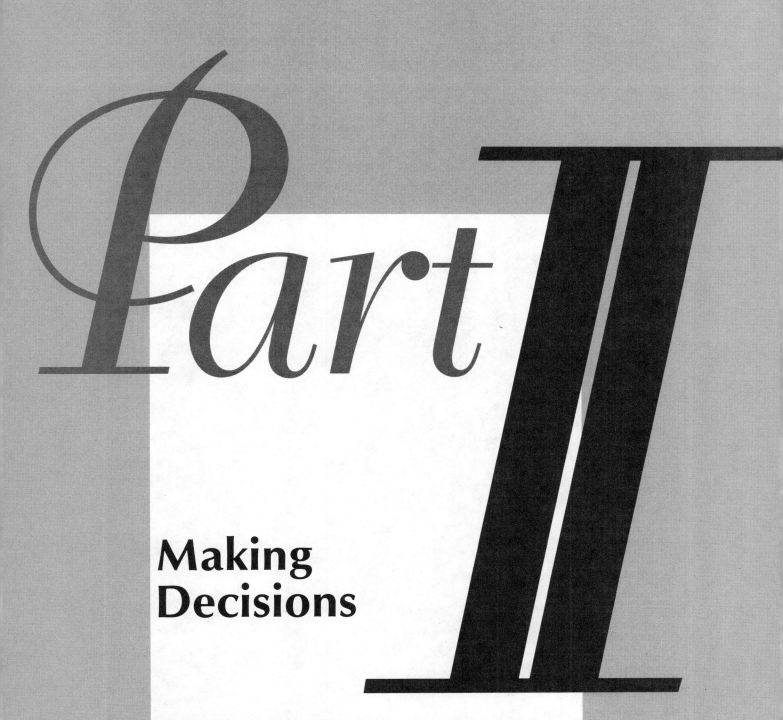

Part II

Making Decisions

Chapter 6

Decisions, Decisions

➤ Key Point

Every day you make decisions. You can think of decisions as problems to solve, actions to take, goals to achieve, or choices to make. You make decisions that affect every aspect of your life.

We should think of decisions in terms of satisfying and unsatisfying rather than in terms of good or bad. Using a logical decision-making process will help you make better decisions that are more satisfying to you.

You Are a Decision Maker

You just made a decision. You decided to pick up this book and read this sentence. You might stop now, or you might read on. You might finish the book and complete all the activities.

If you complete this book, you will find out how to make decisions that are more satisfying to you. You'll learn how to use a step-by-step process to:

- ✔ find the level of importance of a decision
- ✔ get the information you need
- ✔ create more choices for yourself
- ✔ choose the best strategy for you
- ✔ understand the results of different choices
- ✔ tell how well your strategy is working

What will be the result of using this process? The main result will be that you will take more control of your life—all aspects of it.

Easy Decisions

You make thousands of decisions every day, most of them so quickly and easily that you don't even notice they are happening. You may not even think of them as decisions.

Did you brush your teeth this morning? If you did, you made several decisions:

- ✔ Whether to use a toothbrush
- ✔ What kind to use
- ✔ Which one to use
- ✔ Whether to wet the brush with water
- ✔ Whether to use cold water, hot water, or both
- ✔ Whether to use toothpaste
- ✔ What kind to use
- ✔ How much to use
- ✔ Whether to put the cap back on the toothpaste
- ✔ How long to brush
- ✔ How to brush—up and down, back and forth, in circles
- ✔ Whether to rinse
- ✔ Where to put the toothbrush when you finish
- ✔ And so on

You can see that one decision is really made up of many smaller ones. Think about all the little decisions involved in eating breakfast. See if you can list 10 of them below.

1. _____
2. _____
3. _____
4. _____
5. _____
6. _____
7. _____
8. _____
9. _____
10. _____

Chances are you didn't use a step-by-step decision-making process to eat breakfast or brush your teeth. You probably followed your usual routine and acted according to habit.

But suppose that, after you had breakfast and brushed your teeth this morning, you had to decide whether to marry? Whom to marry? Whether to take a new job? Whether to buy a home? How to pay for a home? Whether to have a child? Faced with one or more of these decisions, could you simply follow a routine and act according to habit? Probably not. Since these are important decisions, you would want to think about them, consider alternatives and study results and costs. A step-by-step decision-making process can help you make choices that work for you.

What Is a Decision?

Think of a decision as:

- ✓ a problem to solve
- ✓ an action to take
- ✓ a goal to achieve
- ✓ a choice to make

©1997 JIST Works, Inc., Indianapolis, Ind.

Although we sometimes speak of decisions in terms of "good" or "bad," these are not really useful terms. What might be a "good" decision for one person could be a "bad" one for someone else. Let's replace "good" and "bad" with more useful terms. Think of decisions as being "satisfying" or "unsatisfying."

A satisfying decision is one that produces more satisfying results than unsatisfying results. **"Satisfaction" is determined by you—by your values and preferences.** You are the only one who can place your decisions on a scale from "satisfying" to "unsatisfying."

Levels of Decision Making

Just as decisions come in various sizes and degrees of satisfaction, they also come in different areas.

- ✔ **Everyone makes _personal decisions_.**
  "Should I stay up late to watch this show?"

- ✔ **Everyone makes _educational decisions_.**
  "Do I have enough training for the job I want and the life I want to lead?"

- ✔ **Everyone who works makes _career decisions_.**
  "Should I stay with this job or change to that one?"

- ✔ **Everyone who spends money makes _consumer decisions_.**
  "Can I afford this car?"

- ✔ **Everyone with a family makes _family decisions_.**
  "Do we need a bigger house?"

Decisions in each of these areas come in all sizes and can result in different levels of satisfaction. When you are faced with a decision, the first thing to look at is the level of importance of the decision.

Areas of Importance

A computer program that helps you complete an income tax form is a complex decision-making system. Yet the system is made up of thousands of small decisions that are simple to make. Any major decision:

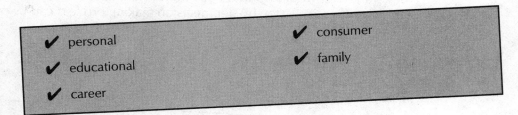

- ✔ personal
- ✔ educational
- ✔ career
- ✔ consumer
- ✔ family

©1997 JIST Works, Inc., Indianapolis, Ind.

is composed of a series of smaller ones. Dividing a major decision into its simpler parts helps make the process easier to understand. The diagram that follows shows four levels of decision making. The explanations after the diagram show that different kinds of information are needed for each level of decision making.

Level 1
Make a Commitment

Level 1 is a decision that reveals your commitment to making a change. It may be hard to face a decision if you're not sure you really want to make a change. *A decision at Level 1 is a yes-or-no proposition: "Will I do something about my situation?"* For this level of decision, you need information about yourself. Do you want to take action? If the answer is "no," you stop here. If the answer is "yes," you have discovered you are committed to action or change, and you move to the next level.

List some Level 1 decisions you have made or now face.

_____
_____
_____
_____
_____

Level 2
Set a Goal

Level 2 involves setting a goal. This is a crucial step. If you are unable to set a goal, you can't make a plan to reach it. *Clarifying your goal makes it much easier to make further decisions.* "I want to work with my hands" is not a clear goal. Should you seek training to become a carpenter or a surgeon, a typist or a sculptor? If you can set a clear goal, you can move on to Level 3. But first you need information about possible goals to set: "What is the right goal for me? How specific should my goal be?"

©1997 JIST Works, Inc., Indianapolis, Ind.

List some Level 2 decisions you have made or now face.

_____
_____
_____
_____

Level 3
Identify Possibilities

Level 3 asks you to identify all the possibilities for accomplishing the goal you set at Level 2. **Expanding the range of alternatives is an important part of making decisions at this level.** For example, if you decided at Level 2 that you want to help children with special needs, you have many possibilities to consider. You could become a physical therapist, a teacher, a researcher, a doctor, a nurse, a fund-raiser, or an inventor. If you want to achieve your goal in other ways, you might use your leisure time to collect for charity, teach sign language, or organize athletic events for children with special needs.

At this level, you need information about all existing possibilities. You need to learn the training requirements and costs for each alternative. You need evidence so you can compare alternatives. After considering the most likely alternatives, you need to identify the one (or ones) most likely to work for you.

List some Level 3 decisions you have made or now face.

_____
_____
_____
_____

Level 4

Take Action

Level 4 is the level of action. **You must plan your action, carry it out, and decide how well it is working.** If you decided at Level 3 that you would try to achieve your goal of helping children by working as a physical therapist, you now have to plan to complete the needed requirements to start your career. You need to choose and complete a training program and prepare for a licensing exam. You need to plan how long this will take, how you will pay for it, and more.

List some Level 4 decisions you have made or now face.

_____

_____

_____

_____

Can you see the importance of each level of making decisions? A person who tries to make a Level 3 or 4 decision before making a commitment (Level 1) or setting a goal (Level 2) is likely to be frustrated. For any major decision, it is important to identify those levels and make your smaller decisions in the right order.

Identifying Levels

NOTE: This set of exercises will give you practice at identifying the different levels of decisions. By the end of the exercise, you will have a clearer idea of where you are with any major decisions you are facing.

Read the following examples of decisions and determine the level of decision each person faces. Write your answer in the space provided.

Here's the Problem ...

1. ____ Max Clark works as a mail sorter for a large company downtown. Most of his day is spent in the basement mailroom, which he calls "the cave." Max has already decided he doesn't want to be a mail sorter for the rest of his life and has begun considering the kind of life he wants to live.

©1997 JIST Works, Inc., Indianapolis, Ind.

2. ____ Matt Rosini, the drama coach at Wilson High School, wants to increase his directing experience. He decides the best way to do this is to direct the Shakespeare series at a summer stock theater. When he calls the theater, the manager tells him to send his application, recommendations, interviews, and list of directing experiences by April 10th.

3. ____ Maria Juarez wants to become a carpenter. There are many avenues open to her: community college, on-the-job training, apprenticeship, and vocational technical school. She must decide which of these she will pursue.

4. ____ Joyce Jefferson works as a researcher for a consulting firm. About twice a month she reads the want ads and makes a note of other companies hiring for similar positions. Her list is growing, but she has yet to follow through on any of the ads.

And the Answer Is ...

1. Max's decision is a Level 2, as he has already committed himself to a change and is considering his goal in life.

2. Matt needs to decide on a plan to complete all the requirements by the April 10th deadline, which is a Level 4 decision.

3. Maria has decided on her goal of becoming a carpenter and now needs to choose the best way to accomplish it, a Level 3 decision.

4. Joyce is not yet committed to change, but is toying with the idea. She needs to make a Level 1 decision—"Will I do something about my situation or not?"

Where Are You?

HINT: To help identify your level of involvement, use the following questions as a guide.

Questionnaire

1. Write down a major decision you are facing.

   _____

2. What prior decisions led you to and will influence this one?

   _____

3. Have you made a commitment to examine your situation?

   _____

4. Can you write your goal in one sentence?

   _____

©1997 JIST Works, Inc., Indianapolis, Ind.

5. Do you have alternatives in mind for accomplishing your goal?

_____

6. Have you devised plans to accomplish your goal?

_____

Key to Questionnaire

Questions 1 and 2

These are intended to help you pinpoint your present decision and place it in context with your past experiences and decisions.

Question 3

If you answered "yes," you are ready to move to Level 2 and start identifying all the alternatives open to you in your chosen field of interest. If you answered "no," you should make a Level 1 decision.

Question 4

If you answered "yes," you are ready to move to Level 3 and start identifying all the alternatives open to you in your chosen field of interest. If you answered "no," you should make a Level 2 decision.

Question 5

If you answered "yes," you can proceed to Level 4 and start taking action. If you answered "no," you should make a Level 3 decision.

Question 6

If you answered "yes," you are ready to begin seeing results from all your work. Congratulations! If you answered "no," you should make a Level 4 decision.

Many people try to answer a Level 3 or 4 decision before completing the Level 1 or 2 decisions. Identifying the levels and completing them in order can be a helpful strategy when you are having trouble making a major decision.

Time Factors

In any decision, time is a factor. How much time do you have to make the decision? How far in the future is the goal you want to achieve? How much time will it take to monitor your strategy for long-range goals?

Time Limitations

Sometimes you have to make a choice in a hurry. If your car goes into a spin, for instance, you have only seconds to decide how to straighten it out. If your career has gone off track, however, or your financial plan needs some adjustment, you have more time to plan for making satisfying decisions.

Your Goals

Suppose you are 25 years old and your financial goals include these: "I want to save $30 by the end of this week and I want to retire by the time I'm 55." The first of these goals—saving $30—requires that you monitor your solution or goal-achievement strategy for only a week. Within a week, you will be able to evaluate your strategy because you'll know whether you've reached your goal.

The retirement goal, however, is a different story. Since the objective is 30 years away, you need a long-range plan. You need to monitor your solution (goal-achievement) strategy for a few decades, not just a few days. Over such a long time, you can expect to make many adjustments to your plan in response to other changes in your life.

So you need to think about time in any decision you make. Ask yourself these questions:

> ✔ "How much time do I have to make the decision?"
>
> ✔ "How far off is the goal?"
>
> ✔ "How long will I have to keep track of my strategy to achieve the goal?"

What Will It Cost You?

Did you know that decisions—even the ones that seem to be free—always cost something? You can't make a decision without paying for it in some way. Some obvious costs include money, time, and energy. If you decide to go skiing on a Saturday, you may spend $75, 10 hours, and most of your energy for the day. But these are not the only costs of your decision. There is also an "opportunity cost." The opportunity cost for any decision includes all the other choices or alternatives you could have chosen but didn't. If you ski on Saturday, you can't go to the museum. You can't visit friends in a different area. You can't do your laundry. You can't work toward achieving other goals. In a minor decision such as this, the things you've given up to go skiing are small sacrifices. But what about major decisions? What are the opportunity costs for the choices that follow?

> ✔ Getting married   ✔ Changing jobs
>
> ✔ Having children   ✔ Moving to a new location

Determining the Cost

In major decisions, opportunity costs also tend to be major. Think of a major decision you've made in your life. In the spaces that follow, write the alternatives you considered, and then the one you finally chose.

Possible Alternatives:

_____
_____
_____
_____
_____

Major Decision:

_____
_____
_____
_____
_____

What If You Had Made a Different Choice?

It's easy to lose sight of how different our lives would be if we had made different choices along the way. We get wrapped up in what we're doing now and don't realize how many ways our decisions affect our daily lives.

Imagine that you had opted for one of the alternative decisions you listed above. How different would your life be now? Write "yes" or "no" in the space provided for each of the following questions.

If you had chosen one of the other alternatives:

_____ Would you be going to the same part of town each day?

_____ Would you be using the same means of transportation?

_____ Would you know different people?

_____ Are there some people you know now whom you might never have met?

_____ Would you be living somewhere else?

_____ Would your career and goals be different?

_____ Would you spend your leisure time differently?

_____ Would your family be different?

_____ In what other ways might your day-to-day life be different?

As a result of all these differences, what other decisions might you be facing now?

_____
_____
_____
_____
_____

What Are the Odds?

We don't need decision-making strategies for certainties, but we do need them for probabilities. There's a possibility that one ticket will win the lottery, but the probability might be 1 in 17 million—not good odds. And odds are what we want to know when a major decision comes up. What are the odds that this alternative will produce a satisfying result? From all the alternatives, which one has the greatest probability of achieving our goals?

In any decision, there is an element of risk or uncertainty. It is important to understand the risks and, if possible, minimize the uncertainties. A good decision-making process helps you identify the risks involved in each alternative. It is important to gather information about risks as you consider alternatives and the possible effects of each one. You can't actually decrease risk by getting information, but you can determine the risks for various alternatives. This process will help you make more satisfying choices.

©1997 JIST Works, Inc., Indianapolis, Ind.

How Much Risk Can You Accept?

How much risk do you like? When it comes to making investments, people vary greatly on the amount of risk they are willing to take. Read the example below and decide which choice you would make. Write your choice and explanation in the spaces provided.

Investment Situation

You have $1,000 to invest. You would be most likely to invest it in which of the following?

- ❏ A guaranteed certificate of deposit that will double your money in seven years

- ❏ A relatively safe stock that could double your money in four years, but that could also decrease in value, leaving you with less than the $1,000

- ❏ A speculative stock that could double your money in a year, but that also could decrease to zero in value, leaving you with nothing

Which one did you choose? Why?

_____

_____

_____

_____

_____

There is no one right choice, although each carries a different level of risk. As is true of almost all decisions, you would have to wait and see how things worked out before you could say if the decision was a satisfying one for you.

©1997 JIST Works, Inc., Indianapolis, Ind.

You Can't Avoid Risk

Remember that avoiding risk is not your goal. Your goal is to discover the risks involved in each of the alternatives available. No matter how much information you get, there will still be some risk.

When you act on your decision, you will have to take a step into the unknown. As you will see in the next section, fear of taking risks can be a real barrier to making decisions. You'll also see that the best way to overcome this fear is to use a decision-making process that gives you the best possible information.

Buying a Car

Suppose you need to buy a car. In this case, you can't afford a new one, so you have to buy a used car. You've seen four cars, and you have different amounts of information about them. The following chart shows how the amount of information you have about each car relates to the amount of risk you will take.

Look at the Risk Chart on the next page. The first row of the chart shows the risks if the car is a bad car. In each case there is some risk of getting a bad car. The important point to note is that, for Car 3 or Car 4, you will probably find out before the sale whether the car is a bad one. For Car 1 or Car 2, the little information you have will probably not tell you if the car is a bad one.

The second row shows the risks if the car is a good one. The risk is low for all four cars, but you would probably find out that it is lower for Car 3 and Car 4.

In reality, represented by the third row on the chart, we can't know ahead of time that cars will be good or bad after we buy them. Yet information is still important. The more information you have, the more likely you are to determine the actual risks. Even with a great deal of information, you will not eliminate risk. You could buy a car that has shown no problems for three years and watch the problems—expensive ones—start the day after you buy it. No mechanic or repair records can guarantee that you'll have no problems.

Information Chart

Car 1 - Rick
Buys the car and knows nothing about it except the make, model, color and price.

Car 2 - Toni
Has information about the mileage, what the car was used for and the repair work that was recently done.

Car 3 - Kim
Has a mechanic check it and tell her what will need repairing soon and what looks in good shape.

Car 4 - Joel
Has the receipts of the work done on the car in the past. Talks to the previous owner and mechanic who worked on it, both of whom are neutral on the sale.

Risk Chart	Car 1 Rick	Car 2 Toni	Car 3 Kim	Car 4 Joel
If the car is a bad car in need of repair	High Risk	High Risk	High Risk	High Risk
If the car is a good car	Low Risk	Low Risk	Low Risk	Low Risk
In real life, we can't know for sure	High Risk	Medium Risk	Medium Risk	Low Risk

©1997 JIST Works, Inc., Indianapolis, Ind.

Checkpoint

Answer these questions:

1. What is a satisfying decision?
2. What are the four levels of decisions?
3. What are the time considerations involved in a decision?
4. How can you overcome the fear of taking a risk?

1. _____
_____
2. _____
_____
3. _____
_____
4. _____
_____

Chapter 7

Obstacles to Making Satisfying Decisions

▶ Key Point

There are many influences on your decisions: your background, your family, your friends and social group, your feelings about yourself. These influences can help you, or they can become internal or external obstacles to making satisfying decisions.

Satisfaction Is Personal

Remember that "good" and "bad" are not useful words to describe decisions. "Satisfying" and "unsatisfying" are more useful because they point to you. You are the judge of how much satisfaction you get from a decision you make. You are the one who sees the results. You are the one who makes the further decisions made necessary by the results.

Influences on Decisions

Although you will be at the center of the decision-making process, you won't be alone in the process. Decision making doesn't happen in a vacuum. The society in which you grew up and now live, your family, your friends and social group, and the way you feel about yourself will all influence the decisions you make.

Think about your own situation. What influences in your life will have an impact on your decisions?

List some of the important influences.

_____
_____
_____
_____

In some cases, these influences will make it easier to find satisfying strategies to reach your goals. A good friend or family member who encourages you can give you confidence and help make the decision-making process easier.

Determining and Defining Obstacles

In other cases, influences may impair your ability to make satisfying decisions. Pressure from a family member, for example, may interfere with thinking about an important change you would like to make. Listen to a few people talk about their conflicts.

©1997 JIST Works, Inc., Indianapolis, Ind.

Some Self-Defeating Statements

- ✔ "I'd like to continue college, but my parents say it's too expensive."
- ✔ "I don't really know what I'd like to do."
- ✔ "I'd like to be a pilot, but it's too hard for women to make it in that field."
- ✔ "I can't. I've got my family to think about."
- ✔ "The reason I haven't decided is that I'm afraid to make a move."
- ✔ "I'd apply for that program, but I know they won't pick someone like me."
- ✔ "I'd do it right now, but my spouse doesn't want to move."
- ✔ "What would my friends think?"
- ✔ "Who would take care of the kids if I went back to school or took that job?"
- ✔ "It's too early. I'm too young."
- ✔ "It's too late. I'm too old."
- ✔ "The time just isn't right."

Do any of these sound familiar? Have you heard any of them before? Have you said any of them before? Among the influences that get in the way of making satisfying decisions, you can be your own worst enemy. You can be the biggest obstacle.

Let's define an obstacle as anything or anyone that prevents you from getting the information you need to take the next step. An obstacle can be present at any level of decision making.

- ✔ At Level 1, a lack of confidence can keep you from making a commitment.
- ✔ At Level 2, age stereotyping can keep you from setting a goal.
- ✔ At Level 3, family pressure can keep you from exploring possibilities.
- ✔ At Level 4, fear of change can prevent you from planning a course of action.

Think of times in your life when obstacles made decisions more difficult. In the spaces that follow, list some obstacles to decisions you had to make (or have to make now).

©1997 JIST Works, Inc., Indianapolis, Ind.

Decision	Obstacle

Internal and External Obstacles

Think of obstacles as either internal (inside of you) or external (outside of you). Sometimes what appears to be an external obstacle is really an internal one.

Internal Obstacles

In one of the self-defeating quotes, the speaker was afraid to make a decision. For this person, fear was an internal obstacle. The people who thought they were too young or too old are also victims of an internal obstacle, the obstacle of self-stereotyping.

If you fear change, lack self-confidence, or think of yourself as too young or too old, your ability to take action is blocked by an internal obstacle.

In the spaces that follow, list some internal obstacles to decisions you had to make (or now have to make).

Decision	Internal Obstacle

©1997 JIST Works, Inc., Indianapolis, Ind.

> ✔ We tend to see what we expect to see. A person who sees him- or herself as a failure will imagine him- or herself failing in a new situation involving risk.
>
> ✔ We tend to see what suits our purposes at a given moment. A hungry shopper in a grocery store tends to buy more food than someone who eats before shopping.
>
> ✔ We see what our backgrounds have prepared us to see. A person whose family is always supportive and encouraging tends to see change more as an opportunity to succeed than as a chance to fail.

Lessons from Psychology:

In order to make a satisfying decision, especially a major one with far-reaching results, you might need to step outside yourself for a while and get a different perspective. A step-by-step decision-making process will help you do this.

External Obstacles

External obstacles can exist in your surroundings or environment. Maria is 32 years old. Her husband has a job that pays well, and their two children are in elementary school. Maria would like to return to work, but she has the rest of the family to think about. If she gets a job, who will do all the things she does now at home?

Robert, a recent graduate from a community college, is 21. He would like to transfer to a four-year school and continue his education, but he doesn't have the money now.

Maria and Robert face external obstacles to decision making. But these external obstacles can also hide or disguise internal obstacles that are the real barriers to decision making. Maria and Robert may really lack the confidence needed to make a commitment to achieving their goals. In other words, the external obstacles may provide handy excuses for avoiding the risks involved in a decision.

Ralph's Dilemma

Look at Ralph's case. As you read the following paragraphs, try to identify the obstacles, both internal and external, that keep Ralph from making a satisfying decision.

Ralph Thompson, a 45-year-old communications specialist, is entering his twentieth year with the Army. At the end of this year, he will be eligible for retirement. Ralph is faced with the decision of whether to stay in his stable and secure position or retire and seek other employment. The only employment option attractive enough to tempt him to give up his position with the Army is that of opening his own radio and TV shop.

There are several things that make Ralph's decision difficult, including some personal characteristics and aspects of his life that have made it easy for Ralph to put off facing this decision for months. On one hand, it would be easy for Ralph to stay in the military and not make a decision. On the other, he really would like to have his own shop, although he is skeptical about his ability to

©1997 JIST Works, Inc., Indianapolis, Ind.

Making Good Career & Life Decisions

start a new career at his age. To complicate matters, Ralph and his family are very comfortable with their present lifestyle and his two teenagers are eagerly anticipating college. There's much at stake for Ralph and his family, and he is afraid of making the wrong decision.

> NOTE: This set of exercises will give you practice at identifying the possible internal and external obstacles that prevent you from making the best possible decision.

Read through the following lists of internal and external obstacles. Check the ones you think are preventing Ralph from realizing his decision.

Internal Obstacles

_____ Fear of making the wrong decision

_____ Fear of taking a risk

_____ Fear of failure

_____ Fear of change

_____ Lack of self-confidence

_____ Ambivalence (having conflicting feelings about the decision)

_____ Procrastination (putting things off)

_____ Stereotyping about self and others with respect to age, race and sex ("I can't do that, I'm too old!" or, "I'm black, or a man, or a woman")*

*Note the difference between stereotyping and self-stereotyping. In one, others do it to you and, in the other, you do it to yourself.

External Obstacles

_____ Family expectations and responsibilities (paying the bills, cooking the meals, feeling pressure not to move, etc.)

_____ Societal stereotyping about age, race and sex ("You can't do that, you're too old!" or, "you're black," or "you're a woman," or "you're a man")

_____ Other societal expectations (pressure to conform, to make more money, to be successful, to be a good parent, etc.)

_____ In some respects, each of these is an obstacle that prevents Ralph from confronting his decision.

Identify Your Obstacles

> REMEMBER: An obstacle is anything or anyone that prevents you from getting the information you need to take the next step.

Use the following exercises to identify obstacles that are keeping you from making satisfying decisions.

©1997 JIST Works, Inc., Indianapolis, Ind.

Pick three major decisions that you recently made or are currently facing. Write them here.

Decision 1:

_____

_____

_____

Decision 2:

_____

_____

_____

Decision 3:

_____

_____

_____

Look at the list of obstacles on the chart that follows. Each can be rated slightly important, moderately important, or very important. (There is no column for "not important" because these problems are almost always present to some degree in a major decision.)

With your Decision 1 in mind, place a "D1" in each column on the chart to rate the importance of each of the obstacles to that decision. Then, go back and do it again for the second decision you thought of, using "D2" this time, and repeat the process for the third decision, using "D3."

Making Good Career & Life Decisions

External Obstacles	Degree of Importance		
	Slightly	Moderately	Very
Family expectation and responsibilities			
Societal stereotyping			
Other societal expectations			
Others:			

External Obstacles	Degree of Importance		
	Slightly	Moderately	Very
Fear of making wrong decision			
Fear of taking a risk			
Fear of failure			
Fear of change			
Lack of self-confidence			
Ambivalence			
Stereotyping about self and others			
Procrastination			
Others:			

©1997 JIST Works, Inc., Indianapolis, Ind.

You might notice some patterns in the obstacles that get in the way of making decisions. Looking at your chart, what would you say are your three most important obstacles to making satisfying decisions?

1. _____
2. _____
3. _____

Identifying these obstacles won't make them disappear, but you must identify them before you can deal with them. Once you know what the obstacles are, you can find specific ways to cope with each one. Remember, we're going to take a large, complex decision and make it easier by breaking it into its parts. Since the obstacles you face are unique to your situation, you are the one who must find strategies to deal with them.

Take Charge of Your Life

Can you think of an area of your life where you have give up some of your responsibility or control? Think of the areas of personal, career, family, education, and consumer decisions. What happens when you give up control?

Before you answer that question, read Susan's story, and try to see the world through her eyes. What does the world look like to Susan? Does she see the source of control over her life as inside of her or outside?

> "I've been overweight for a long time now, and I'm pretty depressed about it. I'm not sure what causes me to be overweight, but I think it started after I had the children. I know that happens to people.
>
> "When I diet for a while, I lose a few pounds, but then something always comes up that makes me go off my diet because I have to eat fattening foods. It seems like there's always a birthday or wedding or party of some sort, or we go out to dinner. Then there's Thanksgiving, and Christmas, and all the holidays. I can't win."

Where is the source of control over Susan's life? She seems to think it lies outside of her, beyond her reach. She is unhappy about being overweight but feels powerless to deal with her problem because she places the control—and the blame—outside herself.

Sometimes people use can't when they really mean won't. This causes several problems for someone such as Susan. First, the feeling of "can't" keeps her from doing something about her problem. She won't make a commitment at Level 1. She won't set a goal at Level 2.

Because she sees no solutions, she won't consider all the possible alternatives at Level 3. Finally, she won't make a plan at Level 4.

What will happen to Susan? She will probably continue to see her problem (and any solutions) as outside of her control.

Susan has given up the power to control her life. By externalizing power and control and responsibility, she has become a willing victim of her circumstances. She doesn't need to continue this way, however. Like any one of us, Susan can take charge of her life and take an active approach to living the rest of it.

Taking Control

Accepting responsibility for your life gives you an active rather than a passive approach to your decisions and your future. Seeing that the source of control can be inside you motivates you to look at your future and think about where you want to go and what you want to do. Taking control means setting goals and planning the steps to reach them.

Problem	*Control Inside/Outside You*
_____	_____
_____	_____
_____	_____
_____	_____
_____	_____
_____	_____

Consider your own situation. In the spaces above, list problems or conflicts you face. For each one, write whether you see control of the problem inside or outside yourself.

When you feel in charge of your life, you are more likely to consider a great number of alternatives and compare the evidence for them. As a result, it's easier to make satisfying decisions. In the next section, you'll see that taking control of your life is an important step in using a decision-making process.

Checkpoint

Answer these questions:

1. What are some external obstacles to making decisions?
2. What are some internal obstacles to making decisions?
3. What can you do about such obstacles?

1. _____
   _____
   _____

2. _____
   _____
   _____

3. _____
   _____
   _____

Chapter 8

Decision-Making Strategies

▶ Key Point

Making satisfying decisions will not eliminate uncertainty in your life, nor is any decision likely to have effects that are 100 percent satisfying. By avoiding time, information, and organization mistakes, you can make more satisfying decisions.

You can make some decisions on your own. When you are unable to make a major decision on your own, get the help you need.

Living with Uncertainty

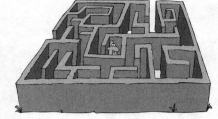

Remember that using a decision-making process will not eliminate uncertainty in your life. In any major decision, any one commitment or goal or course of action may produce satisfying or unsatisfying results. A decision-making process won't let you predict the future, but it will help you gather the right kinds of information—at the right times—to plan for the future as carefully as possible.

Decision-Making Myths

One common idea about decisions is that there are good ones and bad ones. We've already replaced those terms with "satisfying" and unsatisfying."

Can you think of an important decision you made that had all satisfying or all unsatisfying results? These two categories are not enough. Instead of thinking of a decision as satisfying or unsatisfying, think of a range of satisfactions:

Most Satisfying	Least Satisfying

Mostly positive results ─────────────────────────────

├───── **Some positive results** ─────────────────────┤

├──────────── **Some negative results** ──────────┤

├─────────────────── **Mostly negative results**

Some people think confronting a decision means they have to change. Listen to the discussion between Louise and Alice to see different attitudes toward decision making:

Louise: "Have you decided whether to attend the course on career development for women?"

Alice: "No, I haven't. I'm just not sure I want to do anything different from what I'm doing now."

Louise: "That's what the course is for—to help you decide."

Alice: "I know, but I don't want to waste my time and money if I'm not interested in doing something else."

Louise: "It sure wasn't a waste of time and money for me! The course helped me consider my interests, look at all the alternatives, and weigh the evidence. My decision is to continue my life as it was before I took the course, but now I know why I've made that decision."

©1997 JIST Works, Inc., Indianapolis, Ind.

Alice seems to think that unless she wants to change, there is no reason to consider a decision. Louise realizes that facing a decision is not the same thing as ordering a change. She realizes that one of her alternatives is not to change, and she has decided not to make a change.

Avoiding the Usual Mistakes

There are three kinds of mistakes people often make: *mistakes of time, information, and organization.*

Time Mistakes

Time mistakes include procrastinating (putting things off) and jumping the gun (starting too early).

Bill wants to buy a car. He goes to one dealer, looks at three cars, then buys one. Did he act too soon? The answer depends on how satisfying the decision turns out to be. If Bill can afford the car, and the car turns out to be a good one for him, then his timing was good. If he feels later that he should have thought through whether he even needed a car, then he may have acted too quickly.

At the other extreme is the person who never gets around to acting. Putting decisions off rarely eliminates problems, but it does take the person out of the decision-making process. Let's say Bill's new car is making a strange noise. Whenever Bill gives it a little gas, he hears a thumping noise from below the car. The noise doesn't affect the car's performance, so Bill does nothing. He just waits.

Will the car heal itself while he's waiting? No, but in the meantime, he doesn't have to make a decision. By the time he gets around to having a mechanic look at the car, he may be facing a more serious problem and a bigger decision.

Can you think of a decision that was unsatisfying because you did not act at the right time? Describe it below.

Can you think of a decision that was satisfying because you acted at the right time? Describe it below.

Information Mistakes

A person facing a decision may act without enough information or may collect so much information that he or she is buried in details. Think about writing a term paper on the effects of alcohol abuse in the workplace. A writer might find one source and write the paper. This writer makes the mistake of collecting too little information. By using only one source, the writer does not get the benefit of several points of view.

Another writer might consult 50 sources, taking notes from each one. For this writer, there may be too much information. There may be so much data that he or she can't sort out a manageable number of alternatives; in effect, the writer can't see the forest for the trees.

Information mistakes are related to time mistakes. "Too early" may be another way to say "not enough information." There's no simple rule to tell you when it's time to stop gathering information. The question to ask at each level is this: "Do I have enough information for this level?" As you go from Level 1 to Level 4, you need more and different kinds of information at each level.

Can you think of a decision that was unsatisfying because you made an information mistake? Describe it below.

Can you think of a decision that was satisfying because you had the right amount of information? Describe it below.

Organization Mistakes

Too little or too much planning can make a decision impossible or unlikely to produce satisfying results. Once again, there is no simple guideline for how much planning is enough. Think about how much planning is enough for you. Some people like to go out to eat on the spur of the moment: "Let's go to The Lighthouse for dinner tonight." Other people plan such social activities months in advance.

Ted plans his annual vacation about six months in advance, plotting activities ahead of time for each day of the trip. Janet, on the other hand, plans her trip about a week before her vacation. Once she's there, she does what she feels like doing each day—with no plans ahead of time.

Neither is right nor wrong, but either Ted or Jane would probably be uncomfortable on a trip with the other. You have to find the right amount of planning, as well as the right amount of time and information, for you.

Can you think of a decision that was unsatisfying because you planned too much or too little? Describe it below.

_____
_____
_____
_____
_____
_____

Can you think of a decision that was satisfying because you used the right amount of planning? Describe it below.

_____
_____
_____
_____
_____
_____

Developing Confidence

Do you tend to think (and talk) more about your successes than your failures? Are your most memorable moments happy ones or painful ones? When you face a decision, do you anticipate "the thrill of victory" or "the agony of defeat?"

Below, Jesse and Marty talk about an upcoming decision. What is different about their approaches to decision making?

Marty: "Have you decided whether to take advantage of the management training course offered by the company?"

Jesse: "Oh, Marty, I'm just not sure. Are you taking it?"

Marty: "Yes, I plan to. What are you unsure about?"

Jesse: "Well, I know it's a good deal because I researched it to find out how much it would cost to pay for such a course, and about the qualifications of the consultant."

Marty: "So what makes you unsure? Is it the extra time after work?"

Jesse: "No, I don't mind that. I just have trouble making decisions; they usually turn out badly. How can you decide so easily? Decisions aren't so easy for me."

Marty: "They aren't easy for me, either. I figure you have to consider all the facts. Then you need to trust yourself to make the best choice. I'm looking forward to this course and a chance to learn about management."

Jesse: "I guess I'll go to the course because it's such a good deal, but I'm not sure I'll be good at management."

Both Jesse and Marty decide to take the course, but their feelings about the decision are quite different. Marty already feels satisfaction as he anticipates the result of the decision to take the training course. Jesse makes the same decision—to take the course—but feels differently about it. Jesse still isn't positive about the possible outcomes.

Their different expectations may well lead them to different results, or at least different feelings about the results. Marty has a lot of confidence, expects positive results, and will probably focus on the good things that come from taking the course. Jesse has little confidence, expects bad results, and will probably focus on one of two things:

- ✔ The bad things that happen
- ✔ The good things that don't happen

If you identify with Jesse, you may be thinking, "That's fine to suggest that I be self-confident, but I don't have confidence. It's not easy to develop."

You're right—it's not easy to develop confidence. But confidence, like satisfaction, is not an all-or-nothing characteristic. Confidence is a quality people have in varying degrees. You can increase your level of self-confidence by using a decision-making process that helps you focus on the positive.

Catch Yourself Doing Something Right

Start by catching yourself doing something right. Good teachers know that the surest way to help a student is to point out what he or she does well, then suggest the next step. You can use this method to "teach" yourself.

Give yourself credit for each partial success. Start by completing the exercise below. Catch yourself doing something right. Start small; list some minor decisions you've made that you consider satisfying.

Example: Some Good Decisions I Have Made

NOTE: This activity will point out the many satisfying decisions you have already made. None are to be considered insignificant!

Think about the decisions you made recently. It doesn't matter whether these decisions were big or small, satisfying or unsatisfying. Answer the following questions and write your responses in the space provided.

List some good decisions you have made.

_____

_____

_____

_____

_____

_____

Add to your list some major decisions you've made that you consider satisfying.

_____

_____

_____

_____

_____

_____

Ask someone close to you what satisfying daily decisions they've seen you make.

_____
_____
_____
_____
_____
_____

Ask them what satisfying major decisions they have seen you make.

_____
_____
_____
_____
_____
_____

Now, ask someone with whom you have worked (paid/nonpaid) to report satisfying decisions they have seen you make. Ask them for both minor daily decisions and major decisions.

_____
_____
_____

Making Good Career & Life Decisions

_____
_____

If you downplayed your decisions as you were making the list, you missed the point of this activity. The point is to catch yourself doing something right.

Example: Write Yourself a Letter

Sometimes you can gain more objectivity when you look at yourself from someone else's point of view. Try it by writing a letter to yourself about yourself. Use the point of view of an employer (or teacher or friend) writing a letter of praise to an employee (or student or friend) who has just made an important decision.

Use the form that follows to help you write the letter. (N) Write your *name*, (A) write your *address*, (D) write the *decision* you made, (S) write the *setting* in which the decision was made (e.g., family, school, company, community, church), (P) Write the *person* who would be in a position to write this letter (e.g., boss, spouse, friend, teacher). After you finish, read the letter and accept the praise.

(N) _____

(A) _____

Dear (N), _____

The recent decision you made regarding (D)

_____

is another example of your fine contribution to this (S)

_____

It has made significant differences in the following ways:

_____

_____

_____

_____

_____

It is this kind of thinking and action that will help this (S).

_____

continue to develop. I commend you for this decision and for the example you have set for the rest of us in this (S).

_____

Sincerely, _____

(P) _____

©1997 JIST Works, Inc., Indianapolis, Ind.

Praise Yourself

When you make a satisfying decision, however small it seems, be sure to praise yourself; give yourself a pat on the back. Just as you are the central person in making commitments, setting goals, choosing alternatives, and planning actions, you are also the central person for evaluating the decisions you make in your life. You're the one who must decide how satisfying your decisions are.

The best preparation for success is success. If you identify your past successes, even small ones, you can use them as the starting point for future ones. Have you heard the phrase "vicious circle?" There's a happy circle, as well. The happy circle involves success, confidence, and experience.

Recognizing your success gives you confidence. Confidence helps you seek out new experiences. Experience helps you be successful. The new success brings you more confidence. This isn't just a word game. In most sports activities, the way people practice is the way they play. This can be true in other activities as well—activities such as making decisions.

Get Help When You Need It

Some decisions can be made—or must be made—without help. But for most important decisions, you can get help if you want it or need it. How can you tell if you need help? The story that follows shows how people can have different ideas about whether help is needed.

Ms. Cortes: "That's it. We're lost."

Mr. Cortes: "We're not lost. We just go a few more miles to the exit."

Tony (14): "I think we missed it already."

Martha (6): "Are we lost?"

Mr. Cortes: "No. We're not lost."

Ms. Cortes: "We should stop and ask for directions."

Tony: "We should've asked before we got on this road."

Martha: "Does this mean we'll never get there?"

Mr. Cortes: "No! We're not lost. We're on the right road."

Ms. Cortes: "Stop and get directions the next chance you get."

Mr. Cortes: "I'm not stopping. We're going the right way. I can read a map."

If you've ever been in a situation like this, you know that opinions can differ about when it's time to get help. No one in the Cortes family can be sure he or she is right. No one will be able to tell until all of them find out whether they are on the right road. At the time you must make a decision, you may not know whether you're on the right road, either.

©1997 JIST Works, Inc., Indianapolis, Ind.

Think of a situation in your life when opinions differed about getting help. Describe the people involved and their conflicting opinions.

Situation:
_____

People and opinions:
_____
_____
_____
_____
_____
_____

Sources of Help

You can clear up some uncertainty by getting help from others. One level of help is so easy to get that you should probably seek it for any important decision you have to make. This first level includes the people you trust and feel close to: your spouse; a friend; a neighbor; your children; someone who has helped you before; or a counselor, minister, rabbi, or priest.

What can these people do for you when you have to make a decision? Any one of them could help by providing:

- ✔ suggestions of ways to deal with obstacles
- ✔ ideas about possible alternatives
- ✔ opinions about your strengths and weaknesses as they apply to the decision
- ✔ support and encouragement
- ✔ an opportunity for you to hear yourself talk about your ideas

This last benefit may seem like an obvious one, but it is extremely important. When you look in a mirror, you often see a face that's a little different from what you "see" in your mind's eye. If your mind has an eye, it should also have an ear that "hears" you talk to yourself about a problem or decision. Talking aloud to another person, however, lets you hear a different story. Most of us need the audience of another person before we can really listen to ourselves.

©1997 JIST Works, Inc., Indianapolis, Ind.

In the last section of this book, you'll use a decision-making process to help you with an actual decision. Get ready by identifying a number of people close to you who can provide any of the benefits in decision making that were mentioned earlier.

Name: _____

Relationship: _____

Name: _____

Relationship: _____

Name: _____

Relationship: _____

Name: _____

Relationship: _____

Name: _____

Relationship: _____

Name: _____

Relationship: _____

Name: _____

Relationship: _____

Name: _____

Relationship: _____

Name: _____

Relationship: _____

©1997 JIST Works, Inc., Indianapolis, Ind.

There is also professional help available when you need to make an important decision. When medical, legal, or financial advice is necessary, seek it from a qualified person.

In some situations, you might need professional counseling to help you make a commitment, set a goal, explore alternatives, or plan a course of action. When you feel so overwhelmed or anxious about a decision that you are unable to act, a counselor can help. If you just want more information before you act, a counselor or advisor can help. In other words, use help when you know you're lost and when you think there might be a better route.

What can a professional do for you? First, a professional counselor can provide all the benefits listed earlier. Second, a professional is an expert in his or her field, and can give advice that people close to you cannot. Finally, a professional can help you when the people close to you are more a part of the problem than the solution.

Where to Get Help

If you think you might need a professional to help you, here are some sources.

Free Professional Help

- ✔ Community college counseling centers often make counseling available to the entire community.
- ✔ The company or organization for which you work may offer help to employees.
- ✔ Organizations of a wide variety offer services and counseling: women's centers, religious organizations, the American Association for Retired Persons, Forty-Plus Club, and many others.
- ✔ University and college continuing education departments often provide counseling for people.

Professional Help for a Fee

- ✔ Many resources, including many private counselors, charge for their services on a sliding scale based on ability to pay.
- ✔ Community mental health centers offer a variety of counseling: personal, career, values clarification, and goal setting.
- ✔ Many religious organizations offer counseling services (or have a list of referral services) that are not religious but are related to personal concerns and career concerns. Ask what type of counseling they offer and make your needs clear. If you want career counseling, say so.

Career Counseling Agencies

 Professional counselors are people, too. Some will be better or easier to work with than others. When you need help, contact two or three sources. This way, you can get a feeling for the person most likely to work well with you.

Checkpoint

Answer these questions:

1. What are some misconceptions about decision making?
2. What are the usual mistakes people make?
3. Why is it important to catch yourself doing something right?
4. How can others help you make satisfying decisions?

1. _____
   _____

2. _____
   _____

3. _____
   _____

4. _____
   _____

Chapter 9

The Step-by-Step Process

▶ Key Point

The 7-Step Process is the strategy you'll use to make decisions. Your decision-making tactics are the means to move from one step of the process to another.

You can begin by identifying your situation and deciding whether and how you might change it. An important part of the process is expanding the range of alternatives open to you.

Strategy and Tactics

In planning a battle, a military commander must have an overall strategy: *a goal to reach and a means to get there.* Once a strategy is established, however, the battle is not won. What happens when the second step of the strategy doesn't work? You can't call "time out" and start all over again. A commander must plan more than one way to reach a goal and more than one way to go from one step to another within the strategy. Ways of getting from step to step are called tactics. You'll see that the 7-Step Process allows you to use both strategy and tactics when you make your plan of attack for a major decision.

The 7-Step Process

Remember that a big decision is composed of many smaller decisions. Your general plan of attack is to break the decision down into its components and deal with the smaller, more manageable parts. Little by little, you will solve the big problem by solving all of its parts. Here are the seven steps of the decision-making process:

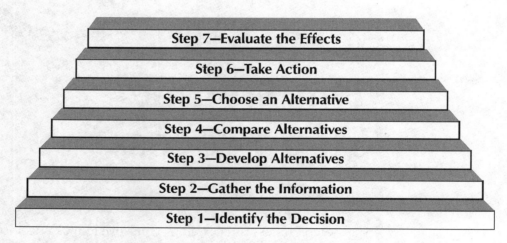

The steps are like a staircase, but they rarely work out in sequence. Several steps may occur at the same time. You may take a step up, realize you need more information, and return to an earlier step. "Gather the Information" appears as a single step, but there are different kinds of information needs at every step.

You're probably wondering how much time it will take to use this process when you have to make a decision. That depends. A person could use all these steps in a few seconds, or could take many years to use them all—depending on the importance and the time requirements of the decision. A doctor in a trauma center may have only seconds to plan and give life-saving treatment to an accident victim whose heart has stopped. At lunch that same day, the doctor may take a few minutes to decide what to order. On her way home that night, she may consider whether she wants to marry the man she's been dating for the past year.

Example: Starting Your Day

Let's take an example of how you've used these steps, perhaps this very morning. After you got up, your decision-making process probably went something like this:

Step 1. Identify the Decision: Time to get dressed.

Step 2. Gather the Information: Working today, find something appropriate.

Step 3. Develop Alternatives: What's clean? Outfits A, B, and C.

Step 4. Compare Alternatives: A is too tight, wore B yesterday, C is okay.

Step 5. Choose an Alternative: Has to be C.

Step 6. Take Action: Put on C.

Step 7. Evaluate the Effects: Look in the mirror. Not bad, not bad.

This whole process, a Level 4 decision, may have happened in a few minutes. You probably didn't take much time at Levels 1, 2, and 3. Did you spend much time discovering a commitment to getting dressed? Setting a goal? Finding alternatives? Probably not. We use this process so often and so automatically that it's almost like breathing; until the going gets really rough, we don't even notice we're doing it.

But for important decisions, we need a different approach. Before going on to see the 7-Step Process in detail, let's consider three ways to look at a decision.

Identify Your Situation—Then Change It

We've all had conflicts to deal with. Every time we make a decision, we face a conflict. The first step of our decision-making model is to identify the problem or decision.

Three Kinds of Conflict

Conflicts come in varying forms. Sometimes you have to choose between two things you want to do. Other times it's necessary to pick the lesser of two evils. A third kind of conflict involves one alternative that has both advantages and disadvantages.

This Looks Good . . . But So Does That

Example — Willie has a schedule conflict. He has to choose between two courses he'd like to take: film studies and speed reading. Since the courses are offered at the same time, he can take only one of the courses.

Analysis — Willie's conflict involves two attractive options. This kind of conflict tends to get solved quickly, as soon as the chooser starts leaning toward one of the alternatives.

Is There a Door Number Three?

Example Willie has another problem with his schedule. This time he has to take one of two courses to fulfill a requirement for graduation, but he doesn't want to take either.

Analysis Now Willie's conflict concerns two equally unattractive choices. The closer he gets to choosing one unpleasant alternative, the worse it looks to him. The tendency for the chooser in this type of conflict is to be driven back to the middle. These conflicts are often resolved at the last minute, when the person is finally forced to make a choice.

Good and Bad Together

Example A third type of conflict occurs when there is only one alternative, but it has both positive and negative qualities. Willie's schedule is full, but his advisor says there is room for him in a one-semester word processing course. Willie thinks, "It's being taught with computers. I'd love to get my hands on a computer, but I'd have to sit there and type for a semester. I could really use the course, though. But I'll have no free time at all for a semester. That means I'll end up doing all my course work at night."

Analysis In this kind of conflict, when there are compelling reasons in favor of a decision and against it, the chooser bounces back and forth. The pleasant aspects of the alternative look better as Willie gets closer to the choice. The negative qualities, however, look worse close up as well, so the chooser is drawn closer and then driven back.

Conflicts of Interest

Read each situation below and decide which type of conflict it represents. Check the appropriate statement.

Case 1 Carlo and Pete are working on a team project that is due on Thursday. Pete didn't come to work on Tuesday or Wednesday. Carlo must either do all the work himself or miss the deadline with the project.

This conflict represents:

_____ Two attractive alternatives

_____ Two negative alternatives

_____ One alternative with positive and negative aspects

Case 2 Alicia's friends are going to a party on Saturday. She had planned to go, too, until Tom asked her to go skiing. Since both events are on Saturday, she can go to only one of them.

This conflict represents:

_____ Two attractive alternatives

_____ Two negative alternatives

_____ One alternative with positive and negative aspects

Case 3 Dante has a job at a restaurant. He works 32 hours each week. He doesn't make much money, but he has a lot of free time. Now he has a chance for a promotion to restaurant manager. The new job would pay much more, but he would have to work 50 hours a week.

This conflict represents:

  _____ Two attractive alternatives

  _____ Two negative alternatives

  _____ One alternative with positive and negative aspects

Conflict Analyses:

Case 1 presents two unpleasant alternatives. Carlo must choose the one that is least unpleasant.

Case 2 offers two attractive alternatives. Alicia will decide which is the better of the two alternatives.

Case 3 involves one alternative with both attractive and unpleasant aspects. Dante's possible job change would have both positive and negative effects.

Expanding Your Options

These cases show common decisions with only two choices. But it is almost always possible to change your situation by expanding the number of alternatives available. The next activity will give you practice in developing choices beyond the apparent limits. Listen to the conversation between Kathy and Ruth about the vacation Ruth's family is planning.

Kathy: "Are you taking a vacation this summer?"

Ruth: "Carl and I decided to take the kids to Ocean City for four days, but we're not too pleased with that decision."

Kathy: "Why are you doing it then?"

Ruth: "It was about our only choice. We couldn't get our vacations together. Mine comes before Carl's and they only overlap four days."

Kathy: "Well, four days are better than none."

Ruth: "I guess so. But we've saved our money and had our hearts set on Miami Beach."

Kathy: "Why don't you go anyway? You and the kids could go early and Carl could come down for four days with all the family together, then he and the kids could stay a few more days. It has some real merit. You'd each have some special time with the kids, you'd have some time together as a family, and you'd each have some quiet time alone at home."

Ruth: "We never even thought of that!"

"I never even thought of that." Have you ever said that? Often we make unsatisfying decisions because we limit ourselves to the obvious alternatives. Perhaps this restricted view comes from approaching real-life decisions as if they are homework assignments. When you have a math problem in school, you assume that all necessary information is given. If you can't solve the problem, you probably think it is your fault: "I have all the information I need, but I just haven't found out how to use it."

But school assignments do not compare well to real-life problems. You cannot assume that all possible alternatives are obvious, or even known, in any given situation.

Ruth and Carl had limited themselves by considering only one vacation alternative. After talking with Kathy, Ruth became aware of another possibility. By developing a new alternative, Ruth increased the probability that the decision will have satisfying results.

Identifying Alternatives

Identifying alternatives is a key step in decision making. In the cases you saw earlier, each person can try to develop new alternatives to get more satisfying results.

Can you think of one more alternative for each case?

Carlo _____

Alicia _____

Dante _____

Two techniques that help in developing alternatives are brainstorming and looking at things differently.

Brainstorming

Brainstorming is the fast, unchecked flow of ideas. Any idea is accepted; no idea is rejected. The rapid flow of ideas brings forth even more ideas, so this activity should be fast-paced and uninterrupted. It helps to brainstorm in a group because one idea will build on another. Try to do some brainstorming for Ruth and Carl. Think about their situation and jot down vacation alternatives for them as fast as you can think of them. Remember: *anything* goes.

_____
_____
_____
_____
_____
_____
_____

Looking at Things Differently

Seeing things through different eyes can also help you expand the range of alternatives in any situation. This technique is based on taking different points of view. You pretend you are someone else and decide what alternatives you would have as that person. In other words, you play "What if . . . ?"

Carl and Ruth might look through the eyes of a single parent with the same vacation schedule. Either of them might think of alternatives such as these:

- ✔ Spending a few days with the children at a place they choose and a few days at a resort with a friend while the children stay with Aunt Nancy.
- ✔ Spending a few days with the children and a few days alone at a resort while the children stay with a live-in baby-sitter.
- ✔ Sending the kids to camp and having the time at home alone.

Carl and Ruth can seek other points of view. Pretending they are newlyweds with only four days for a honeymoon, they consider these options:

- ✔ Spending four days in a hideaway cottage in the mountains.
- ✔ Heading for Miami for three nights of exciting night life.
- ✔ Relaxing at a nearby beach.

When they come back to reality, they might combine and compromise with ideas from some of the new alternatives. They might decide to have the children stay with Aunt Nancy while they enjoy four days in the mountain cottage. You can probably think of other views Ruth and Carl could take to help them see things from different points of view.

But can you see things from other points of view when you have a decision of your own to make? We can often see alternatives and solutions for others that we cannot see for ourselves. Sometimes we are too close to our own situations to see them from any other point of view.

When you are feeling this way, think of someone you know who had a similar decision to make, and consider the alternatives that person came up with. Another technique is to step outside yourself for a moment and pretend you are your own best friend. Give yourself the friendly advice you would give any friend in similar circumstances. By doing so, you may see other alternatives open to you. Practice by trying the activity that follows.

Developing Alternatives

NOTE: With this activity, you will use the various strategies discussed for developing possible alternatives to determine the best course of action for making a more satisfying decision.

Think of a decision you are facing. Select one that must be made soon and that you are willing to discuss with others: List the alternatives you've already considered.

Next, use brainstorming to expand your list. If you can, enlist the help of a family member or friend. List everything that comes to mind, and don't discuss any of the items—just expand the list.

Now try seeing your situation through other eyes to discover still more alternatives. List the new alternatives below. Think of yourself as your own best friend.

Compare and combine your expanded lists of alternatives to write the best possible solution to the decision you have to make.

_____

The Process in Action

Earlier, you learned about the four levels of decision making:

Level 1. Make a commitment
Level 2. Set a goal
Level 3. Identify possibilities
Level 4. Take action

Jerry's Story

Read the story that follows to see how one person moves through these levels, combining them with the 7-Step Process to make a satisfying decision about a career change. Jerry Price, a 28-year-old insurance agent, is married to Gail, also 28, a secretary. Their two children are 5 and 3 years old. Jerry has been unhappy with his job for some time. About two months ago, he talked to his friend Paul and began investigating job possibilities at another local agency.

> "I'm just not happy. It's hard to get up and go to work in the morning. I watch the clock most of the day because I don't really like my job. When I get home, I'm out of patience, and I feel like I'm taking out my troubles on the rest of the family. I've got to do something.

"When I talked to Paul about it, he told me about the job at the other agency in town. I don't like the way they do things there. Paul says I want too much. Maybe he's right. I've got a job here that pays well, and I'm slowly working my way up in the company. I'd have to give up a lot to move now. Gail wouldn't like that idea very much. The problem is, I'm not happy here."

Step 1. Identify the Decision

What can Jerry do? He has recognized the warning signs that he needs to make a decision: tension, anxiety, boredom, frustration, moodiness. In the 7-Step Process, he's still at Step 1 (identify the decision). So far, he hasn't made a Level 1 decision (making a commitment).

"I've got to do something. I can't face another two years of doing this job. I'm going to start looking for something else."

Step 2. Gather the Information

"What do I need? I need a job of equal or higher pay in the insurance business, but I want something with more variety and responsibility. And less paperwork!"

Analysis. Jerry is beginning to gather information for alternative job possibilities. He has made a Level 2 decision by setting a goal.

"It's going to be tough to decide ahead of time what job will make me happy. There are lots of other jobs, but how many of them pay enough? How many am I qualified for? How many of them could I take without selling the house and moving? How can I be sure I won't be worse off after a change than I am now?"

Analysis. Jerry needs information for this Level 3 decision (finding alternatives). He's worried about salary and qualifications, and these worries won't go away until he gets some facts. He needs to consider the following:

- ✔ Information about himself, most of which he already has: interests, skills, values, lifestyle preferences, and goals.
- ✔ Information about other jobs, most of which he doesn't have: job descriptions, work settings, job characteristics, coworkers, salary, status, requirements for education and training, and more.
- ✔ Information about people close to him, some of which he has: who should be considered, how they feel, how his decision will affect them, and how they might affect the decision.

©1997 JIST Works, Inc., Indianapolis, Ind.

Jerry organizes his ideas by putting them on the chart on the below.

Now he needs to get that information from various sources. He visits the personnel office at his own company and finds a list of all positions, including salaries of each. He talks to people he knows in some of the positions. He uses supportive personal relationships by talking with his family and his friend.

"Paul has known me for a long time. He's the one who got me thinking about making a change. I was worried about bringing up this idea with Gail. I thought it might look like a crazy, dangerous idea. After all, my present job is pretty secure."

Information I Need

Facts About Myself
- ✔ Which of my values must be satisfied at work?
- ✔ What kind of work do I want to do?
- ✔ What lifestyle do I want?

Facts About Alternatives
- ✔ What alternatives are open to me?
- ✔ Which alternatives am I most qualified for?
- ✔ What salary do I need?
- ✔ What additional preparation will I need for each alternative?
- ✔ What do I like about my present job?

Feelings About Significant People

Person	How decision affects person's feelings	How person's feelings affect decision
Gail	If I am unhappy, it will affect our relationship.	She must agree with my decision.
The Children	They might suffer financially.	Their opinion is important.
Paul	Not significant.	His opinion of me could change.

Step 3. Develop Alternatives

"When I finally talked to Gail, she surprised me. She'd known I was unhappy. She works, too, so she knows how important this is. She had some ideas that no one else thought of."

Analysis. Jerry has overcome some obstacles by using supportive relationships. Now he's ready to develop a list of alternatives. At Step 3 (developing alternatives), Jerry might describe the decision like this: "If I change jobs, what job should I change to?" At this step, he should be opening up the scope of his research.

Step 4. Compare Alternatives

"I crossed out jobs I didn't know much about, but Gail told me I was ruling things out too early."

Analysis. Jerry is developing a list of jobs that fit his criteria of being in the insurance business and at a similar salary level. He arrives at Step 4 ready to compare the alternatives. He lists pros and cons for alternatives.

"I don't feel like I'm closer to a decision. I wanted a job in insurance at the same pay but with more variety and less paperwork. I need to look at more than just pros and cons for each job. I need to think about short-term and long-term effects, the risks involved, what I can do, and what I like to do."

Analysis. Jerry talks to Paul and Gail about satisfying events in his life. He remembers that he enjoyed tutoring students, speaking to groups, working with his children, and explaining his company's policies to clients. In short, he likes to teach people. This discovery pushes him take a closer look at two of his alternatives: campus recruiter and personnel instructor.

When thinking about risks, Jerry considers losing his job security, including his seniority, fringe benefits, and company retirement. He realizes that to evaluate the alternatives, he needs to rate the importance of certain job characteristics.

- ✔ Family or friends support this choice
- ✔ High enough status
- ✔ Limited travel requirements
- ✔ Nice variety of tasks
- ✔ Financial security
- ✔ Much paperwork
- ✔ Work with people
- ✔ Limited responsibility
- ✔ Few decisions to make
- ✔ More education required

©1997 JIST Works, Inc., Indianapolis, Ind.

Making Good Career & Life Decisions

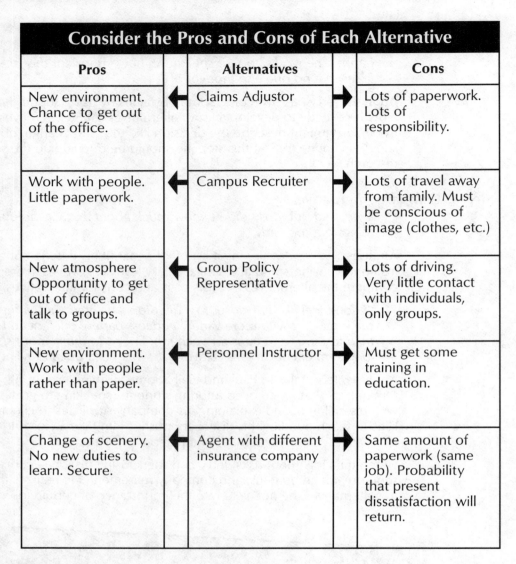

Consider the Pros and Cons of Each Alternative

Pros	Alternatives	Cons
New environment. Chance to get out of the office.	Claims Adjustor	Lots of paperwork. Lots of responsibility.
Work with people. Little paperwork.	Campus Recruiter	Lots of travel away from family. Must be conscious of image (clothes, etc.)
New atmosphere. Opportunity to get out of office and talk to groups.	Group Policy Representative	Lots of driving. Very little contact with individuals, only groups.
New environment. Work with people rather than paper.	Personnel Instructor	Must get some training in education.
Change of scenery. No new duties to learn. Secure.	Agent with different insurance company	Same amount of paperwork (same job). Probability that present dissatisfaction will return.

Using a Weight Chart

Jerry decides to pick one of the jobs he's considering and try doing a weight chart for it. He's going to consider two things:

✔ The degree of importance each characteristic has

✔ The likelihood of encountering the characteristic on the job

First, Jerry rates the importance of each characteristic. If it's very important, he gives it a 4. If it's slightly important, he gives it a 2. If it's not very important, he gives it a 0.

Next, Jerry rates the likelihood of encountering each characteristic. If it's very likely, he gives it a 4. If it's somewhat likely, he gives it a 2. If it's not very likely, he gives it a 0.

The next step is to multiply the degree of importance by the likelihood of encountering each characteristic. Look at Jerry's sample chart below. The first one, "family or friends will be supportive," was slightly important to Jerry, so he gave it a 2. He decided that the likelihood of family or friends being supportive for that job rated a 4. He multiplied these two numbers and wrote in the total in the last column, under "Total." Jerry completed the rest of the chart following the same process for each characteristic. Then he added up the Total column. He filled out a chart like this for each of five job alternatives he was considering.

Jerry also noticed how many times the number 16 appeared in the Total column of his charts for each job. A 16 meant that the job characteristic was very important (scoring a 4), and that the likelihood of encountering that characteristic was very high (scoring another 4). Comparing the totals and the number of 16s for each job alternative gave Jerry a clear picture of which job seemed most suited to his needs.

Job Alternative: Personnel Instructor		
Job Characteristics	**Degree of Importance x Likelihood of Encountering**	**Total**
Family or friends will be supportive	2 x 4	8
Status	2 x 2	4
Travel requirements	2 x 0	0
Variety of tasks	4 x 4	16
Financial security	4 x 4	16
Great deal of paperwork	0 x 2	0
Work with people	4 x 4	16
Limited amount of responsibility	4 x 2	8
Few decisions to make	2 x 4	8
Additional education required	2 x 2	4
	Total	**80**
	Number of times total is 16	**3**

Degree of Importance
4 = Very Important
2 = Somewhat Important
0 = Not Very Important

Likelihood of Encountering
4 = Very Likely
2 = Somewhat Likely
0 = Not Very Likely

©1997 JIST Works, Inc., Indianapolis, Ind.

Step 5. Choose an Alternative

Now, Jerry has a numerical solution. Personnel instructor produces the highest total and the most 16s, and if he follows the numbers, that's the job for him. Before he goes to Step 6 and takes action, however, he should consider once more how this choice matches his feelings. After talking it over with the people who have helped him so far, Jerry takes the responsibility and makes his choice.

"Well, that's it. I want to be a personnel instructor. I need to set up a time table for acting on each part of my plan."

Analysis: Now Jerry has a Level 4 decision to make. He has to plan and follow a course of action (Step 6 in the decision-making process). Acting on a decision cannot be as hard as taking all the other steps in the process.

Step 6. Take Action

Jerry begins by dividing his plan into parts. First, he will find out if he needs more training. Then he'll learn the job application procedures. After this, he will compare this position in different companies, including his own.

Step 7. Evaluate the Effects

Where will Jerry end up? As he gathers information and tries to put his plan into action, there may be more changes. He might find out about another job that interests him. His environment may change. The company may reorganize and create a position for a director of training, an ideal job for Jerry. It's important to remember that a decision can be modified. People change and situations change.

Eventually, Jerry can evaluate the effects of his decision. This is Step 7 in the decision-making process. Whether his decision turns out to be very satisfying, very unsatisfying, or somewhere in between, Jerry has taken control of his life and left a job he did not like. He can always use what he has learned in this process to make new decisions.

In the next chapter, you will put this step-by-step process into action for yourself, to see how this process works for you.

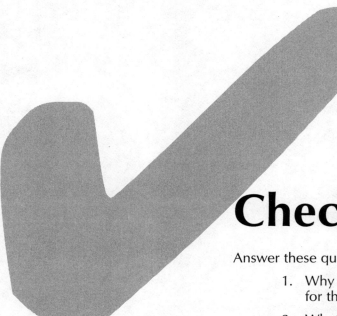

Checkpoint

Answer these questions:

1. Why do you need both strategy and tactics for the decision-making process?

2. What are the seven steps in the process?

3. What are ways to develop new alternatives?

1. _____
   _____
   _____

2. _____
   _____
   _____

3. _____
   _____
   _____

Chapter 10

Using the Process

> ### *Key Point*

When you evaluate your earlier decisions, you should see what steps in the process produced the unsatisfying decisions and then pay careful attention to those steps in your next decision.

You can use the 7-Step Process to plan, carry out, and evaluate important decisions for the rest of your life.

Making Good Career & Life Decisions

Look at Your Past Decisions

Earlier, you saw some mistakes people typically make when they face major decisions. Before you use the 7-Step Process to work your way through a decision of your own, review how you handled some important decisions in the past.

On the charts that follow, make evaluations of two or three important decisions you faced in the past few years. Complete each area as indicated by naming the decision, describing the decision, and checking the appropriate boxes.

Evaluation Charts

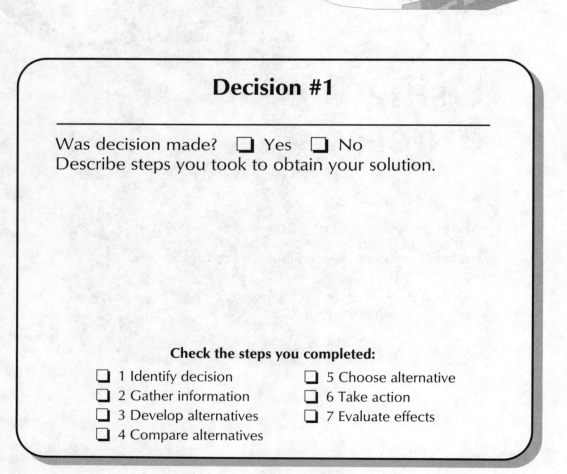

Decision #1

_____

Was decision made? ❏ Yes ❏ No
Describe steps you took to obtain your solution.

Check the steps you completed:

❏ 1 Identify decision   ❏ 5 Choose alternative
❏ 2 Gather information   ❏ 6 Take action
❏ 3 Develop alternatives   ❏ 7 Evaluate effects
❏ 4 Compare alternatives

©1997 JIST Works, Inc., Indianapolis, Ind.

Decision #2

Was decision made? ☐ Yes ☐ No
Describe steps you took to obtain your solution.

Check the steps you completed:
☐ 1 Identify decision   ☐ 5 Choose alternative
☐ 2 Gather information   ☐ 6 Take action
☐ 3 Develop alternatives   ☐ 7 Evaluate effects
☐ 4 Compare alternatives

Decision #3

Was decision made? ☐ Yes ☐ No
Describe steps you took to obtain your solution.

Check the steps you completed:
☐ 1 Identify decision   ☐ 5 Choose alternative
☐ 2 Gather information   ☐ 6 Take action
☐ 3 Develop alternatives   ☐ 7 Evaluate effects
☐ 4 Compare alternatives

©1997 JIST Works, Inc., Indianapolis, Ind.

Are there steps you left out of past decisions? If so, which ones did you tend to leave out?

Are there steps you tried that didn't work well? Which ones?

Can you see a pattern in the charts on the previous pages? As you prepare to make a decision, are there steps you need to reconsider? If so, return to "Levels of Decision Making" and review how to make a commitment, set a goal, develop alternatives, and get help when you need it.

Make Your Decision

NOTE: This activity is designed to help you use the 7-Step Process to make a decision. Remember, these steps often overlap.

The following exercises can be used in several ways. Depending on the complexity of the decision and your experience in using the 7-Step Process, you may wish to:

- ✔ use only the detailed worksheets
- ✔ use only the summary chart
- ✔ use both the worksheets and the summary chart

Step 1. Identify the Decision

Step 2. Gather the Information

Information I need in order to make this decision.	
Facts about self	*Example.* Interest, values, preferences, goals, obstacles
Facts about possible alternatives	*Example of a career decision.* Job characteristics, skills
Facts about significant people (family and friends)	*Example.* Who should be considered? How could my decision affect them? What effects do their feelings have on my decision?

©1997 JIST Works, Inc., Indianapolis, Ind.

Step 3. Develop Alternatives

Remember to use this step to expand alternatives. You can eliminate later, but first provide yourself with a long list from which to choose.

List the alternatives you have already considered.

Use brainstorming and "trying on hats" to add to the list.

Use supportive relationships to help you expand the list.

```
┌─────────────────────────────────────────────────┐
│  _____    │
│                                                 │
│  _____    │
│                                                 │
│  _____    │
│                                                 │
│  _____    │
│                                                 │
│  _____    │
│                                                 │
│  _____    │
│                                                 │
│  _____    │
└─────────────────────────────────────────────────┘
```

Step 4. Compare Alternatives

List the alternatives you have identified and consider the pros and cons of each. Project possible results of each alternative.

If considering pros and cons is not enough to enable you to choose an alternative, you can use the numerical weighing system Jerry used to compare alternatives. The decision-making charts on the next pages will help you do so.

Across the top, write one alternative you are considering. In the first column, list the characteristics that are important to you.

In the second column, rate the degree of importance of that characteristic (4 for very important, 2 for somewhat important, 0 for not very important) and multiply it by the likelihood of encountering it in that job (4 for very likely, 2 for somewhat likely, 0 for not very likely). Go back and look at Jerry's chart in the previous chapter if you need to. Write the total in the "Total" column. Add up the Total column at the bottom, and also notice how many times you got a 16.

Job Alternative #1:		
Job Characteristic	Degree of Importance x Likelihood of Encountering	Total
	Total	
	Number of times total is 16	

Degree of Importance
4 = Very Important
2 = Somewhat Important
0 = Not Very Important

Likelihood of Encountering
4 = Very Likely
2 = Somewhat Likely
0 = Not Very Likely

Job Alternative #2:

Job Characteristic	Degree of Importance x Likelihood of Encountering	Total
Total		
Number of times total is 16		

Degree of Importance
4 = Very Important
2 = Somewhat Important
0 = Not Very Important

Likelihood of Encountering
4 = Very Likely
2 = Somewhat Likely
0 = Not Very Likely

©1997 JIST Works, Inc., Indianapolis, Ind.

Job Alternative #3:		
Job Characteristic	Degree of Importance x Likelihood of Encountering	Total
	Total	
	Number of times total is 16	

Degree of Importance
4 = Very Important
2 = Somewhat Important
0 = Not Very Important

Likelihood of Encountering
4 = Very Likely
2 = Somewhat Likely
0 = Not Very Likely

Job Alternative #4:

Job Characteristic	Degree of Importance x Likelihood of Encountering	Total
	Total	
	Number of times total is 16	

Degree of Importance
4 = Very Important
2 = Somewhat Important
0 = Not Very Important

Likelihood of Encountering
4 = Very Likely
2 = Somewhat Likely
0 = Not Very Likely

©1997 JIST Works, Inc., Indianapolis, Ind.

Which alternatives have the highest totals?

Which alternatives have the most 16s?

These charts aren't going to make the decision for you, but they will help you make it.

Step 5. Choose an Alternative

Are you ready for Step 5, choosing an alternative?

If You're Not Ready . . .

What kinds of additional information do you need?

What obstacles are in the way of this decision?

Do you need to backtrack and expand your range of alternatives? What additional alternatives can you think of?

Making Good Career & Life Decisions

If You Are Ready ...
Which alternative do you choose?

```
_____
_____
_____
_____
```

Step 6. Take Action

Scheduling the parts of your plan on a time line or chart will help you to set intermediate goals on the way to achieving the main goal.

Decide what intermediate steps are needed to complete your plan of action. Arrange these steps in the order in which they should happen. Then assign dates for completion of each step. Write your plan in the space provided.

Intermediate steps in plan of action	Completion target date

©1997 JIST Works, Inc., Indianapolis, Ind.

Step 7. Evaluate the Effects

In the last step of the decision-making process, you evaluate the effects of the decision. This process can last for a short or a long time, depending on the importance and range of the goal. Here are some questions to help you review your plan of action while you still have time to change it.

> ✔ Do you have new information that tells you to adjust anything in your original decision?
>
> ✔ In the original situation?
>
> ✔ In the goal?
>
> ✔ In the alternatives?
>
> ✔ In the plan of action? The intermediate steps? The timing?

As you monitor the effectiveness of your plan, remember that there are no good or bad decisions—only decisions that are satisfying or unsatisfying to you. You are weighing positive and negative results. A decision that has more positive effects than negative ones should be considered a satisfying decision.

Use the following summary chart to see all the steps you followed in making this decision.

Summary Chart of Your Decision

The flow chart that follows will help you summarize the decision you want to make by presenting it visually in logical order. Keep in mind the four levels involved in effective decision making.

Making Good Career & Life Decisions

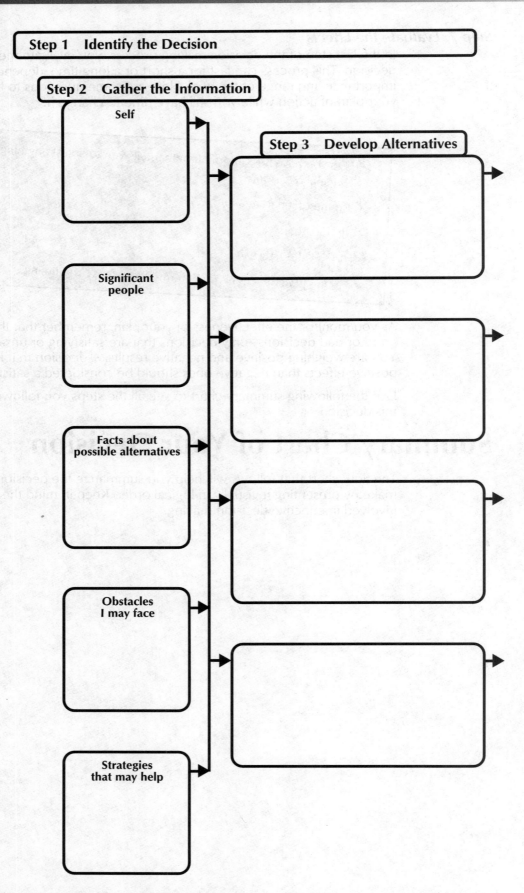

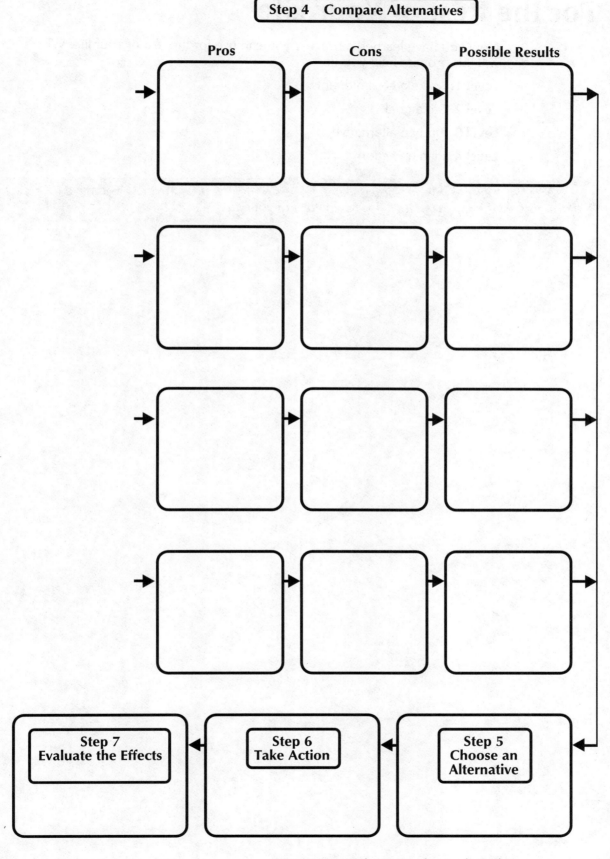

For the Rest of Your Life

Now you have learned a process you can use for the rest of your life. What will this process help you do?

Level 1. Make a commitment

Level 2. Set a goal

Level 3. Find an alternative

Level 4. Plan an action

NOTE: You can use this decision-making process to help you do anything you have to do—and anything you want to do—for the rest of your life.

Chapter 10 Using the Process

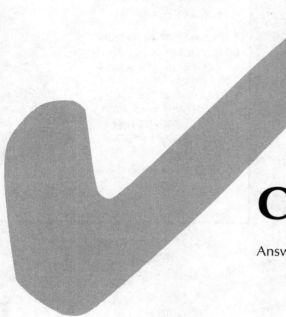

Checkpoint

Answer these questions:

1. What can you discover about your method by looking at your past decisions?

2. How can you compare alternatives?

3. Where might you adjust your plan of action?

1. _____

2. _____

3. _____

More Good JIST Books

How to Get a Job Now!
Six Easy Steps to Getting a Better Job
J. Michael Farr

Read this book in the morning and substantially increase your job search effectiveness that afternoon. Thousands of employment programs and over a million individuals have used these same methods to find better jobs and found them in less time.

ISBN 1-56370-290-8
$6.95
Order Code J2908

Getting the Job You Really Want
3rd Edition
A Step-by-Step Guide
J. Michael Farr

The best book of its kind! A unique, interactive job search and career planning guide. This book helps readers through the entire career selection and job search process. Used in programs across North America.

ISBN 1-56370-092-1
$9.95
Order Code RWR

The Quick Resume & Cover Letter Book
Write and Use an Effective Resume in Only One Day
J. Michael Farr

America's leading job search and career guidance expert has created the definitive guide to resumes. Includes a special "Same Day Resume" section, plus tips on searching for jobs, interviewing, cover and follow-up letters, and much more.

ISBN 1-56370-141-3   **$12.95**   Order Code RCLQG

Selected by Publishers Marketing Association as one of the top three business books of the year!

Gallery of Best Resumes
A Collection of Quality Resumes by Professional Resume Writers
David F. Noble

The author invited members of the Professional Association of Resume Writers to submit their best designs for review. This book is the result—a "best of the best" collection of 200 top resumes, plus invaluable resume writing tips from the experts.

ISBN 1-56370-144-8
$16.95
Order Code GBR

The Right Job for You, 2nd Edition
An Interactive Career Planning Guide
J. Michael Farr

With so many career options, selecting a course for the future can be a daunting task. This book makes it easy. Its interactive approach helps readers assess their strengths and interests and steers them toward career choices that make sense!

ISBN 1-56370-286-X
$9.95
Order Code J286X

To order these and other JIST products, call your local bookstore or distributor. Please call 1-800-JIST-USA for complete information about our exceptional product line.